LETTING GOD COME CLOSE

3/8/ '04
BLESSED AND HAPPY
DAY AND YEAR
LOVE,
Bob

OTHER BOOKS BY WILLIAM A. BARRY, S.J.

LETTING GOD
COME CLOSE

AN APPROACH TO THE IGNATIAN SPIRITUAL EXERCISES

WILLIAM A. BARRY, S. J.

an imprint of
Loyola Press

Chicago

an imprint of

Loyola Press
3441 North Ashland Avenue
Chicago, Illinois 60657

This book is a revised and expanded edition of a work titled *Allowing the Creator to Deal with the Creature: An Approach to the Spiritual Exercises of Ignatius of Loyola* (New York: Paulist Press, 1994).

The Scripture quotations contained herein are from the New Revised Standard Version Bible: Catholic edition, copyright © 1993 and 1989 by the Division of Christian Education of the National Council of the Churches of Christ in the U.S.A. Used by permission. All rights reserved.

Acknowledgments continued on p. 204

Interior design by Amy Evans McClure
Cover Design by Kathy Kikkert
Cover Photograph by Joshua Sheldon

Library of Congress Cataloging-in-Publication Data
Barry, William A.
    Letting God come close : an approach to the Ignatian spiritual exercises / William A. Barry.
        p. cm.
    Rev. ed. of: Allowing the creator to deal with the creature. c1994.
    Includes bibliographical references.
    ISBN 0-8294-1684-6
    1. Ignatius, of Loyola, Saint, 1491–1556. Exercitia spiritualia. 2. Spiritual exercises. I. Barry, William A. Allowing the creator to deal with the creature. II. Title.

BX2179.L8 B36 2001
248.3—dc21   2001038030

Printed in Canada
03 04 05 06 07 08 09 Webcom 9 8 7 6 5 4 3 2

In grateful memory of

Sister Mary Agnes Reed, R.S.M.,

Who, as Sister Mary Nativity,

Taught me at Sacred Heart Grammar School,

Worcester, Massachusetts,

And with great love and fidelity prayed for and cared for

Me and all those whom she taught

Until the day of her death,

Holy Saturday, April 10, 1993.

CONTENTS

PREFACE

After the Second Vatican Council, many religious orders and congregations began to reclaim their heritage, going back to their founders to rekindle the original charism that had led to the foundation of their orders or congregations. It was no different for the Society of Jesus. One discovery the Society made was that the Spiritual Exercises of their founder, Ignatius of Loyola, had originally been given to individuals, not to groups. Prior to 1965, the notion of individually directed Exercises was almost unheard of and had been unheard of, it seems, for more than a century. In living memory, Jesuits and others knew nothing of a tradition of individually directed retreats. The Spiritual Exercises were preached to large groups of people, and they had an enormous impact in this form. So pervasive was this practice that some Jesuits felt the introduction of the individually directed retreat was an innovation, and perhaps an unhealthy one at that, another instance of the triumph of psychology in spiritual matters.

After 1965, Jesuits and others began to learn how to give the Spiritual Exercises to individuals. Training courses and programs proliferated. People flocked in large numbers to retreat houses to make individually directed retreats of varying lengths up to the traditional thirty days. At first, these people were largely diocesan priests and men and women who belonged to religious congregations, but gradually word spread among the Catholic laity and then to members of other Christian churches. Now there are a number of retreat houses in the United States that almost exclusively give directed retreats throughout the year. In addition, the rediscovery of the Ignatian heritage has led to the giving of the Spiritual Exercises to individuals and small groups while these people carry on their ordinary daily lives. On any given day in the United States, hundreds of people are making the Exercises by praying for an hour and a half every day and seeing their director once a week while continuing to work a regular job and carry out their other daily tasks.

As a result of this recovery of the tradition, the Spiritual Exercises have taken on a new life in the church. Articles and books have appeared at a steady rate, climaxing in 1991 during the five hundredth anniversary of the birth of Ignatius. Since 1970, I have been engaged in giving the Exercises, in training directors of the Exercises, and in writing on various aspects of Ignatian spirituality. During the Ignatian year, I gave a series of lectures on the Exercises at Boston College, and this series was published in 1991 by Ave Maria Press as *Finding God in All Things: A Companion to the Spiritual Exercises of St. Ignatius.* That book tries to make the Exercises accessible to people with the hope that many more will want to try them out under direction. The present book has a different focus. My hope is that it will be helpful to directors, either by stimulating their own creative directing or by being a foil against which they can joust to deepen people's understanding and experience of this tremendous tool. I have reworked material already published in journals and have added new material, all of which tries to show how I approach directing the Exercises. I hope that the book may also be helpful to people who seek God, who want to let the Creator deal immediately with them. All my writing aims to help people who hunger for God, to encourage them to give God a chance to satisfy that hunger.

I have dedicated the book to Sister Mary Agnes Reed, R.S.M., who taught me in grade school and who always kept me in her heart and thoughts throughout her life.

She died on Holy Saturday afternoon, 1993. As it turned out, I was putting the finishing touches on the first draft of this book as she lay dying and then died. Let her stand for all those dedicated Sisters of Mercy who helped shape my early years both intellectually and religiously. I am grateful to them all.

I thank my father and sisters, who so faithfully read my material and encourage me. Once again I am indebted to Marika Geoghegan, my good friend, who read the manuscript and gave me strong encouragement. My community of ten other Jesuits has been a great help to me since I became provincial two years ago. Without them, I would not be able to do my job, nor would I have the time and energy to write. Moreover, they encourage me in my writing. I am especially grateful to William C. Russell, S.J., and William G. Devine, S.J., who read the first draft very quickly and thoroughly, gave me helpful suggestions for improving it, and expressed enthusiasm for the material. Finally, I take this opportunity to thank the past and present staff of the Center for Religious Development in Cambridge, Massachusetts, who helped me to hone my approach to spiritual direction and to the direction of the Exercises and who encouraged me to write in those early days of learning how to direct the Exercises.

Preface to the Revised Edition

I am grateful to Loyola Press and to my editor there, Linda Schlafer, for agreeing to reprint the book. For this reprint I have made some changes in order to remove duplications and inconsistencies and to bring the book more up-to-date. I have also enlarged the last chapter on the Contemplation to Attain Love and have added a chapter on the historical Jesus and the Second Week. I hope that the book will continue to enlighten people on God's ways of dealing directly with us.

William A. Barry, S.J.
January 2001
Laus Deo Semper!

One Approach to Allowing "the Creator to Deal Immediately with the Creature and the Creature with Its Creator and Lord"

In the Fifteenth Introductory Explanation to the Spiritual Exercises, Ignatius urges the director to maintain equilibrium with regard to the choices a person making the Exercises faces. At the end of the paragraph, he says,

> Accordingly, the one giving the Exercises ought not to lean or incline in either direction but rather, while standing by like the pointer of a scale in equilibrium, to allow the Creator to deal immediately with the creature and the creature with its Creator and Lord. [n. 15]

In this first chapter, I want to outline how I approach directing the full Exercises in the form commonly called the "thirty-day Ignatian retreat." In other words, I want to present how I try "to allow the Creator to deal immediately with the creature and the creature with its Creator and Lord." To introduce my approach, let me cite Gilles Cusson.

> We shall speak of the "integral" Exercises. This expression does not necessarily refer to the matter of time, that is, to the "thirty-day retreat." In fact, the making of the Exercises does not derive its value principally from the framework in which they are given, nor from the precision of details and their technical apparatus. Their authenticity is measured, instead, by the quality of the spiritual experience which they foster, by their helping the retreatants to prepare themselves for the salutary encounter with God, in Christ.[1]

This strong statement echoes my own convictions. The Spiritual Exercises contain a method of encountering God's action in our universe in an ordered progression. People who have the prerequisites and desires can let God strip them of their inordinate affections so that they can find God's will and thus become more and more attuned to God's redemptive intention in creating this universe. Ignatius himself cites the purpose of his Spiritual Exercises as overcoming "oneself, and to order one's life, without reaching a decision through some disordered affection" [n. 21]. For Ignatius, union with God meant union with a God who is always actively bringing about God's reign in this universe. Union with God meant ordered desires and action.[2]

My own practice of giving the full Spiritual Exercises has evolved over a period of about thirty years, so I will describe it here as succinctly as possible. I have directed individuals in retreats of varying lengths, both in the city and in country retreat houses. The clientele has also varied, from Jesuits to Roman Catholic sisters, Catholic and non-Catholic laypeople, ministers and priests. My approach has been honed in peer group supervision with other directors. It has also undoubtedly been affected by my training as a clinical psychologist, by my work as a training supervisor of spiritual directors, and, of course, by my upbringing in the United States of America as the son of immigrant Irish parents. The extent to which this approach fits with the approaches of Jesuits and others from widely different cultures remains to be seen. I present my own approach with the hope that others will find it helpful, if only as a foil against which to test their own ways of proceeding.

The Principle and Foundation

I assume that the Exercises will be profitable for people in proportion to the depth of their desires, a topic that we will take up explicitly in chapter 2. Those who are ready for the full Exercises must, I believe, have strong desires to develop and deepen their relationship with God. Such desires, if they are real, are based on strong, positive experiences of God, experiences that I have come to call the affective Principle and Foundation. This may be better understood if I first describe people who do not have such positive experiences of God. These are the fearful, scrupulous people whose image of God seems to be one of a tyrant. The British psychoanalyst Harry Guntrip notes:

> It is a common experience in psychotherapy to find patients who fear and hate God, a God who, in the words of J. S. Mackenzie, "is always snooping around after sinners," and who "becomes an outsize of the threatening parent. . . . The child grows up fearing evil rather than loving good; afraid of vice rather than in love with virtue."[3]

Pierre Favre, one of the founding members of the Society of Jesus, seems to have been in this condition when Ignatius first met him in Paris. It would be four years before Pierre would be ready for the full Exercises, after much patient spiritual direction by Ignatius. What the Favres of this world need in order to desire closeness to God and detachment from their inordinate desires is an experience of the enjoyment of God such as that described by the psychiatrist J. S. Mackenzie.

> The *enjoyment of God* should be the supreme end of spiritual technique; and it is in that enjoyment of God that we feel not only saved in the Evangelical sense, but safe: we are conscious of belonging to God, and hence are never alone; and, to the degree we have these two, hostile feelings disappear. . . . In that relationship Nature seems friendly and homely; even its vast spaces instead of eliciting a sense of terror speak of the infinite love; and the nearer beauty becomes the garment with which the Almighty clothes Himself.[4]

Such experiences of the "enjoyment of God" elicit the desire to get to know God better and to let one's life be governed by one's relationship with God.

Another way to describe this affective Principle and Foundation is to point to experiences of desiring "we know not what," periods of great well-being accompanied by a yearning for Mystery itself. Sebastian Moore describes such occasions, explaining them as experiences of God's desiring us into being.

These experiences of our creation immerse us in a great desire for the consummation of God's own intention for the universe and for each one of us.[5] C. S. Lewis calls this desire "Joy,"[6] an intense longing that is distinguished from other longings by two things. "In the first place, though the sense of want is acute and even painful, yet the mere wanting is felt to be somehow a delight. . . . This hunger is better than any other fullness; this poverty better than all other wealth." Second, we can be mistaken about the object of the desire, as Lewis himself was for a good part of his early life. Lewis concludes,

> It appeared to me therefore that if a man diligently followed this desire, pursuing the false objects until their falsity appeared and then resolutely abandoning them, he must come out at last into the clear knowledge that the human soul was made to enjoy some object that is never fully given—nay, cannot even be imagined as given—in our present mode of subjective and spatio-temporal experience.[7]

I believe that Ignatius spells out the implications of such an experience in the First Principle and Foundation.[8]

When people have such an affective Principle and Foundation, they desire to be united with God and to know God's dream for them and for the universe.

Before I agree to direct someone in the full Exercises, I try to ascertain whether he or she has had sufficient positive experiences of God such that this desire is present. In the first couple of days of the retreat, I suggest exercises that will bring back to memory these experiences of being desired into existence and kept in existence by a loving Creator who has a dream for that person. Psalms such as 8, 104, and 139 are proposed for prayer. I often suggest a day of prayer in which the person asks God to reveal her personal salvation history. After expressing the desire for such a personal revelation, she recalls a person, a place, or an incident of early childhood and then lets the associations rise freely, trusting that among the influences on her memories will be God's Holy Spirit. She can concentrate on later periods of her life in other periods of prayer on the same day. The purpose is that she experience anew and in depth God's loving creation and providence for her and for the whole universe, along with the heartfelt knowledge that she has a part to play in it, and a desire to know what that part is.

No matter how meticulously one tries to screen people prior to beginning the full Exercises, some people begin them without a deep trust in God. In such cases, the time spent on the affective Principle and Foundation can take a number of days. One man, a Jesuit for more than fifteen years, spent about ten days struggling with whether or not he could entrust his life to the God who had, seemingly, let him down early in his life. It was time well spent; indeed, the lack of trust might not have come to consciousness if he had not been making the full Exercises with a director. Without this foundation, however, it makes no sense to try to move the person to the next stage of the Exercises. The Exercises are an ordered progression in which one stage depends on the relatively "successful" completion of the prior stage, and the whole edifice depends on the solidity of the foundation.[9] If the foundation is not firmly established prior to beginning the full Exercises, then the wise director has no alternative but to help the retreatant to allow God to build it firmly at that time.

I hope that it is already apparent that the kind of direction I do and encourage in others requires the ability to listen to the experience of the directee and to adapt one's approach accordingly. The director, in other words, must have developed some of the basic listening skills of a good counselor, such as the ability to help the other to be concrete and somewhat detailed about experience, the ability to respond to the directee with accurate empathy, and the ability to

ask questions for clarification in a way that does not
imply a negative judgment on the other person's
experience.[10] Very often, directors need much help
and supervision to overcome their tendency to want
to give answers or to help the person to discern before
the actual experience of the person is sufficiently
explored. Before discernment is possible, they must
become sufficiently aware of their own experiences.
Directors who too quickly presume that they know
what their directees have experienced run the risk of not
permitting "the Creator to deal immediately with the
creature and the creature with its Creator and Lord"
[n. 15] and thus of leading them astray. Later in the
chapter, I will return to the topic of supervision.

The First Week

People who have a profound experience of the
affective Principle and Foundation recognize that
God is creating this universe so that all men and
women might live in harmony with the Trinity and
in community with one another. They also realize
that each person has a role to play in God's loving
intention for this universe. Such people will want to
live out God's plan, but they also know that the
world and they themselves are not in harmony with

it. Such felt knowledge leads to the First Week of the Spiritual Exercises, in which the desire is to know how both they and the world have fallen short of what God intends. At the same time, they want to know that God has not given up on them or on the world. One can put the desire this way: "I want God to reveal to me how God sees me and my world."

The novelist Brian Moore captured this desire well at the end of his novel *Black Robe*. The novel is set in Canada at the time of the French conquest of the Native Americans and poignantly describes the clash of alien cultures as the French Jesuit priests try to convert the Iroquois and the Hurons. The protagonist, Pére Laforgue, has witnessed this tragic clash, has himself been tortured by the Iroquois, and has at times doubted the existence of God. At the end of the novel, he is baptizing people of the Huron tribe, knowing that their baptism will mean the end of their civilization. The novel thus depicts both personal and cultural brokenness and sinfulness. It ends with these words: "And a prayer came to him, a true prayer at last. 'Spare them. Spare them, O Lord. Do you love us?' 'Yes.'"[11] That prayer of Père Laforgue and the response to it express some of the desire of the person who enters the dynamic of the First Week of the Spiritual Exercises.

In the course of the First Week, I try to help people to look not only at their own sinfulness and sinful tendencies but also at the history of sin in the world. The first meditation on Triple Sin can be given as it is in the book of the Exercises, but they can also meditate on the condition of the world at present and then reflect on the historical conditions that have contributed to the present conditions. The headlines of the day's newspapers can often supply the opening for such reflection. The seemingly intractable evils of our day portrayed in the newspapers bring home the power of evil and of the Evil One and show how far from the intention of God our world has strayed. Such a meditation can also bring home the sense of hope-lessness people may harbor with regard to such social evil and thus lead to the desire to be freed from this. I also suggest that they ask God to reveal their own complicity in this history of sin and evil in the world in a period of prayer that complements the earlier period when they asked God to reveal their salvation history.

During this First Week, I also propose Scripture texts that might help them to face God and Jesus as the sinners they are. Examples are the woman caught in adultery (John 8:1–11), the Israelites in exile because of their sins (Isaiah 43:1–7), the washing of the feet (John 13:1–11), and Peter's triple profession of love (John 21:15–19). During this time, I suggest that they end their prayer periods by looking at Jesus on the cross and speaking directly to him. It is quite difficult for many people who are aware of their sinfulness to look directly into the eyes of Jesus on the cross, but when they do, they come to a deep realization of his love and forgiveness. During this time, they also pray the triple colloquy suggested by Ignatius, first asking Mary to intercede with Jesus, then asking Jesus to intercede with his Father, and finally begging the Father for a deep knowledge of their own sins and sinful tendencies as well as of the disorder of the world in which they live [n. 63]. This triple intercession indicates the depth of their desire for freedom from all sins, sinful tendencies, and inordinate attachments.

In directing this Week of the Exercises, I have assumed that only God can reveal our sins and sinful tendencies to us. Sin is precisely a blind spot that keeps us from knowing ourselves as we really are. So we beg God for God's view of ourselves and of our world so that we can repent and try to live out God's dream for us and for our world in cooperation with God's grace. Actually, in each of the weeks of the Exercises, the *id quod volo,* the desire, is for a personal revelation of God, as we shall see in more detail in chapter 3. I shall allude to the object of this desire in each of the weeks.

During this First Week, people who have long harbored the deep-seated fear that some secret sins, some sinful tendencies, or something of which they are ashamed could not bear the light of day, or somehow would not be forgiven by God, can find themselves freed from an overwhelming burden. Let one example suffice for many. Suppose someone has for years feared that he is a homosexual. With his rational mind he can tell himself that God loves him no matter what his erotic attractions may be, but he cannot admit to God exactly what these attractions are because he fears that God will repudiate him. As long as these fears keep him from being open with God, his prayer experiences will be somewhat superficial. God will seem distant, and the director will notice that his description of prayer seems dry and intellectual. There will not be much of the kind of movement that Ignatius expects during the Exercises.

The alert director can help the directee by questioning him about his desires and about how he feels about the way the prayer periods are going. If director and directee have established a good working relationship, the director can point out that the person's prayer seems dry and overly rational. By judicious questioning and gentle confrontation, the director can help the person to recognize that something is keeping him from closeness to God. He may realize, in the course of further prayer, what that something is. During this Week, he has a chance to pour out to God and to Jesus the content of both his fears and his fantasies and to discover that God still looks on him with love and care. This experience can disabuse him of the illusion that God's love is conditional and can lead him to the freedom from self-absorption that makes entrance into the Second Week of the Spiritual Exercises possible and desirable.

I hope that during this Week, retreatants will also realize that God loves this real world with all its sinful and corrupting social structures. In other words, during this period in the Exercises, people can come to the deep realization that God wants the world itself to be more of a place where men and women can live out God's dream for them. God has not given up on the world, in spite of all the horrors perpetrated in it, in spite of the injustice and poverty, the murders and torture so easily verified by a casual reading of the newspaper headlines. During this Week of the Exercises, retreatants can come to recognize God's revulsion at the social injustice in the world while at the same time experiencing God's tremendous love for our world and for our feeble efforts to live out God's dream.

The Second Week

I look upon the Kingdom meditation as an exercise that evokes the deep-seated desire in us for the fulfillment of God's dream for the world. It also evokes our desire for someone to whom we can give our whole selves in order to fulfill that dream. The parable of the earthly king is of a piece with the myths of the hero and heroine that have been a part of world literature since its inception. The prophecies of the Jewish Scriptures that evoke our hopes in Advent are also of this type. The early Christians read these prophecies and then pointed to Jesus as more than fulfilling them. In a sense, the way a person reacts to these myths indicates whether or not he or she has the desire of the Second Week.

Let me give an example using Luke 4:16–21. In this section, Jesus reads from the prophet Isaiah in the synagogue and then says, "Today this scripture has been fulfilled in your hearing" (Luke 4:21). If, upon hearing these words of Isaiah, a person focuses on herself as one of those in need of healing or freedom rather than on the figure of Jesus who has a mission, then perhaps she is still in the dynamic of the First Week; the focus is still on her need for healing and forgiveness. But if she thrills at the program of the prophet and wants to be with Jesus on his mission, then she has the desire of the Second Week, which is the desire for Jesus to reveal himself to her so that she may love him more and follow him more closely. In chapter 5, we will explore more deeply the transition points to the four weeks.

During the Second Week, I begin with the First Day proposed by Ignatius. The contemplation of the Incarnation, with its reference to the Trinity looking down upon the world, brings back to mind both the Principle and Foundation and the First Week. The contemplation of the Nativity, with its suggestions for the colloquy, looks forward to the Passion and cross. After this first day, I usually suggest a day spent on the first ten chapters of Mark's Gospel. People rarely read a whole Gospel in one sitting, and Mark's first ten chapters can be read reflectively in less than one prayer period. During the other prayer periods of the day, they can go back to those aspects of Jesus' life, ministry, and personality that struck them most forcefully. For the next day or two, I suggest a closer look at scenes from the first three chapters, culminating in the call of the Twelve.

He went up the mountain and called to him those whom he wanted, and they came to him. And he appointed twelve, whom he also named apostles, to be with him, and to be sent out to proclaim the message, and to have authority to cast out demons. (Mark 3:13–15)

For most retreatants, these days lead to the question of whether or not they want to ask to be chosen, as the Twelve were chosen, to be companions of Jesus. They are then ready to take a day to meditate on the value systems of Satan and of Jesus, which is Ignatius's Fourth Day. Stripped of the medieval imagery, the meditation on the Two Standards strikes a responsive chord in people. Woody Allen's *Crimes and Misdemeanors,* for example, depicts the progression of temptation. In that movie, an honored doctor comes to the point of hiring an assassin to kill his mistress because she threatens to spill the beans to his wife. Reputation and money are on the line; hence, he assumes the role of God and pays the assassin to kill her. Herod's banquet in Mark 6 also depicts the same progression. Rather than lose face among his guests, Herod finally kills John the Baptist, although it is something he does not want to do. In this meditation, Ignatius again suggests a triple colloquy, praying first to Mary, then to Jesus, and finally to the Father [n. 147]. This triple prayer underlines the reality that these two value systems square off in battle within the individual heart. If we are to live by the values of Jesus, we absolutely need the grace of God; we need to be put under the value system of Jesus by the Father. The meditation on the Three Classes of Persons finishes this Fourth Day.

For the rest of the Second Week, I usually suggest the section of Mark's Gospel from 8:22 to the end of chapter 10. This section can be looked at as an *inclusio* because it begins and ends with the healing of a blind man. Moreover, Bartimaeus, after his cure, "followed" Jesus "on the way," the way that leads to Calvary. In this section, Jesus predicts his passion three times, and three times the disciples are blind. Jesus also speaks of the costs of discipleship. During these days, retreatants continue to ask to know Jesus in order to love him more and follow him more closely, and they continue to pray the triple colloquy of the meditation on the Two Standards.

The issue before them is how Jesus wants them to live out their lives as disciples. I take the "election" as an issue of God's election of the person and not, in the first instance, as an issue of the election or choice by the retreatant. This stance is also supported by Leo Bakker.

> The exercitant does not stand before a whole row of objects of election from among which he must choose those which agree more with God's will; rather, according to Ignatius, the exercitant who wants "more" actually finds himself facing only one alternative: a life in which he only *desires* to take on the likeness of his earthly Lord, or a life in which he may *actually* take on this likeness. Election—the grace of the Second Week—is, therefore, nothing else than the inner knowledge of the Lord in order to love him more and to follow him more closely.[12]

In other words, retreatants face the question, Does God want me to live out my life as a disciple of the poor Jesus? If the answer is yes, the concrete details of how to live out this choice can only be worked out after the conclusion of the Exercises.

Of course, at this time of election a person may conclude that God's election or call to follow the poor Christ includes a concrete way of living, as a religious or as a lay missionary, for example. But the concrete details may not work out. At Manresa, for example, Ignatius himself came to the conclusion that God wanted him to work to "help souls" in poverty. He also wrongly concluded that Jerusalem was to be the venue of his apostolate. Life after Manresa eventually taught Ignatius the concrete way in which God's election of him would enflesh itself. During the Exercises, another young man came to a profound knowledge and love of the poor Jesus and to a conviction that Jesus was calling him to apostolic work. He also concluded that Jesus was calling him to enter the Jesuits. But the Jesuits, for some reason, did not accept him, and he had to look further to see how to concretize his election. Directors need to be aware of the difference between the election to discipleship and the concrete details of a life of such discipleship, which can only be worked out in a world where many factors come into play.

The Third and Fourth Weeks

The Third Week is ushered in by the aroused desire in the person making the Exercises to have Jesus reveal what his passion and death were like. In the First Week, the retreatant looked at Jesus on the cross, but the desire then was to know that Jesus still looked on her, the sinner, with love. The focus was more on her needs. Now the focus is on Jesus and on what he is suffering. The desire is for compassion for Jesus. Even those who have this desire may be surprised, however, at how difficult it is to stay with

Jesus in contemplation of the passion. But it could hardly be otherwise. All of us shy away from pain, suffering, and death. If we find it very difficult to face our own suffering and eventual death, we often find it even more difficult to face the suffering and death of those we love.

We do not easily ask our loved ones to tell us what they are suffering, and we put off mentioning to them the reality of their imminent death as long as possible. When people enter the Third Week, these dynamics are operating even though the desire to share Christ's sufferings is very strong. Directors need to recognize how deep the resistance is and help their directees face it without getting discouraged. Nowhere else in the Exercises is it so clear that consolation does not necessarily mean feeling happy and content. I have known people who have suffered deeply during this Week as they have felt not only what Jesus himself suffered but also what he still suffers in all the sufferings of the people of our world. Yet painful though it was, they knew that they wanted to stay close to Jesus and found themselves desolate when they pulled away from contemplation of his sufferings.

The Fourth Week arrives with the desire to have Jesus reveal the joy of his resurrected life. Here, too, it may not be easy for the person to stay with the contemplation of the risen Jesus. I believe that one source of resistance here is the hidden hope that with the Resurrection, the cross and death of Jesus will be seen as only a bad dream. But the risen Jesus carries the marks of his passion on him. The past is not undone. The wisdom of Jesus is hard to accept; namely, that he could only be the risen One he now is through the actual life he led and the death he suffered. "Oh, how foolish you are, and how slow of heart to believe all that the prophets have declared! Was it not necessary that the Messiah should suffer these things and then enter into his glory?" (Luke 24:25–26). The only way to have the joy of the Resurrection is to accept it as a grace on God's terms.

Another source of resistance, I believe, is a deep-seated reluctance to surrender ourselves totally to God. It is difficult to accept the fragility and frailty of all the best efforts of our lives and to leave Resurrection and the success of the kingdom to the Father. It is very hard to believe in practice that the only way to save our life is to lose it and that the only way to enjoy life is to not cling to it with might and main. Again, retreatants need to be reminded that they desire a grace and that this is not something within their power to bring about.

Often in a thirty-day retreat, not much time is left to spend on the Contemplation to Attain Love. I will have more to say about this in chapter 11. If this contemplation gets shortchanged, I usually point it out and suggest that retreatants might want to continue with it after the retreat is over. I explain that it is a contemplation, not a meditation. We are asking here for an intimate knowledge of God's great gifts. In Manresa, Ignatius had a number of mystical experiences, which he describes in his *Autobiography*. These seem to have been the experiential substratum for the Contemplation. Ignatius hopes that the exercitant will experience God's creative touch, God's desire and efforts to share with us as much of himself as he can. In effect, Ignatius hopes that the exercitant will experience the whole world and every moment in it as sacred, as "charged with the grandeur of God."[13]

Ignatius himself seems to have realized that directors need to be reminded to let the Creator deal directly with the creature. Both in my own practice and in supervising others, I have come to realize that reminders are often not enough. Directors too easily fall into wanting to help with counsel or theology or directions, especially when their directees are experiencing difficulty. In the actual direction session, directors reveal that their faith in the reality of God's direct dealings with their directees is rather weak. Moreover, in the intensity of the one-to-one direction, personality patterns in them and in their directees are activated. Transference and counter-transference reactions often occur. These can be expected to be rather strong in a thirty-day retreat in which the director and directee meet every day and deal with very intimate experiences.

As a result, groups of directors with whom I have worked have tried to engage in some kind of super-vision. Most often, the directors gather regularly for peer supervision in a group setting. The focus of such supervision is not on the absent party (the retreatant) but on the experience of the director. The director presents her experience of directing someone, revealing her own reactions and thoughts and feelings. The peer group helps her to examine her experience and to understand why she is reacting as she is. Directors are encouraged to present experiences that trouble or concern or surprise them. In this way, they can learn something about themselves as directors and can also see where they need to request God's help to become better directors.[14]

Conclusion

In this chapter, I have tried to show how I approach the direction of the Spiritual Exercises. Ignatius discovered in his own experience that both God and he could deal directly with each other and that these dealings had an ordered progression. Perhaps because of my training as a psychologist, I tend to see this ordered progression in terms of an ever-deepening relationship analogous to the development of an intimate human relationship. Any developing intimate relationship between two humans begins with an initial attraction (the affective Principle and Foundation). As the relationship develops, it will gradually erode the egocentric concerns of both of the parties and shift both to a concern and care for the other instead of the self (First Week). Moreover, if such a developing relationship continues to unfold authentically, it will lead the two people to larger concerns than just their own (Second Week). Finally, people in an intimate relationship must come to grips with suffering and death (Third Week) in order to fully enjoy life itself (Fourth Week). The human analogy, however, pales before the reality of what happens when the Creator deals directly with the creature and the creature with his or her Creator.

CHAPTER 2

"What Do You Want?": The Role of Desires in Prayer

"You're going to ask what I want." "As I was driving up to the retreat house, I thought of your perennial question: 'What do you want?' and here's what I came up with." I have often noticed that people who see me for some time for spiritual direction or directed retreats say things like this. It even becomes a bit of a humorous byplay, as though they want to beat me to the punch. Clearly, one of my favorite questions for directees is the one Jesus put to the two disciples who began to follow him, "What are you looking for?" (John 1:38). If they pick up on this predilection and start asking themselves the question, then, I believe, a good deal of my work as spiritual director is done. If we know what we want in prayer, we are going to find our way. After a practical belief that God wants an intimate relationship with each one of us and that God is directly encountered in our experience, nothing is more important for the development of our relationship with God than knowledge of what we want and of what God wants. In this chapter, I want to discuss the role of desires in prayer.

Anyone familiar with the Spiritual Exercises knows that among the preludes to every meditation or contemplation is the instruction "to ask God our Lord for what I want and desire." In the various stages or weeks of the Exercises, Ignatius states what the desire is to be in each case. For example, in the First Week, I "ask for growing and intense sorrow and tears for my sins," and in the Second Week, I "ask for an interior knowledge of Our Lord, who became human for me, that I may love him more intensely and follow him more closely." In chapter 3, I will show that each of the desires of the Exercises is a desire for some particular revelation by the Lord.

On the face of it, it looks as though Ignatius is saying, "Here is what you should desire at each stage of the Spiritual Exercises." If a director interprets it this way, he or she might take a person through the four Weeks and simply put before him or her what

Ignatius gives as the desire. In fact, this has been the procedure in preached retreats, including the preached thirty-day retreats we older Jesuits and other religious made in our novitiate. But what happened if, as a matter of fact, I did not really desire to know Jesus more intimately when the Second Week was presented to me? Suppose, for example, I was still too afraid of what he thinks of me. In most instances, I would guess, we just presumed that we had the desire if it was time for the Second Week. But I contend that without the real desire, we never got very intimate with Jesus. Indeed, I believe that "what we really desire" is diagnostic of the stage of the Exercises we are actually in. To demonstrate this thesis, we need to look at the role of desires in any relationship.

If we get a call from someone requesting a meeting, isn't our first question, at least to ourselves, "What does she or he want?" In fact, many meetings come off badly because the individuals involved have mistaken ideas of what each person wants. Perhaps I want to become someone's friend, and he believes that I want help with my computer; he wants to help me but is not even thinking of a deeper friendship. At the end of the meeting, both of us are going to be pretty frustrated unless we talk about our different desires and come to some understanding. Often enough, relationships become frustrating because of ambivalent or incompatible desires. For example, I want to get closer to a woman, but I am also afraid of her. Or I want a friendship with her (a happily married woman), but I also want to have an affair. Every intended encounter with another person is accompanied by a desire or desires. We are not always aware of our desires, but they are present, and they condition our behavior in the encounter.

Now suppose that I want to befriend someone, and he does not want my friendship. Will my efforts to befriend him get either of us anywhere? Only to frustration and resentment, most likely. And what will happen if I persist in trying to do nice things for him? He will probably get more and more irritated and thus less and less likely to become my friend. And like many a do-gooder whose good deeds are rejected, I may eventually wash my hands of him and call him an ingrate who deserves his fate. Friendship is only possible when the desires are mutual, when he freely desires my friendship and I freely desire his. Friendship cannot be coerced.

"But," someone may object, "we often do things that we do not want to do. Because of my friendship with you, for example, I will go to a movie I don't like." But what does this person want? If it is because of her friendship with me that she goes to the movie, her deepest desire is to please me or to be with me, is it not? The friendship is more important than the movie. I believe that the centrality of desire for the developing of a relationship cannot be denied.

Now let us look at the importance of desires in the relationship with the Lord. In the first chapter of John's Gospel, the two disciples of John are intrigued by this Jesus whom John has just pointed out as the Lamb of God. So they start following Jesus. When Jesus asks them what they are looking for, they say, "Rabbi, where are you staying?" They do not yet have strong desires; curiosity seems to be the desire. Jesus does not disdain this desire: "Come and see." Unless we have some attraction toward God, some curiosity or hope or desire, we will not take the time to begin our side of the relationship. If we believe in our hearts and minds that God is an ogre, ready to pounce on us for any infraction, then we may try to placate God, but we will never want to get close to God. And God, as it were, bends over backward to convince us that God really is benign, that God really is, as Jesus asserted, Abba (dear Father, or because God has no gender, dear Mother).

The profligate wonders of nature, our own creation and life, the words of the Old and New Testaments, Jesus himself, and the influence of loving, caring people in our lives—these are all signs of God's desire that we find God attractive and let God come close. But God cannot, or will not, force us into closeness. We must have some desire to get to know God better. Sebastian Moore affirms that the creative touch of God that desires us into being arouses in us a desire for "I know not what"; that is, a desire for the Mystery we call God.[1] This experience (understood as the experience of one's creation and continued creation) can be seen as the affective Principle and Foundation for the development of one's relationship with God. The desire for "I know not what" is what makes our hearts restless until they rest in God.

Many people need help to recognize that they have such a desire. Because of life's hurts, they may not recognize any other desire than to be left alone or not to be hurt anymore. Telling such people that God is love has little or no effect. They may need help to let God know that they are afraid and desire to be less afraid. Indeed, they may need help to voice some of their anger at life's hurts, especially when they believe these hurts have come from the Author of life. The fact that they have not completely turned away from religion indicates that they may still want something from God, even if only an acknowledgment that God knows what has happened to them in life. Like Job, some may cry out, "know then that God has put me in the wrong, and closed his net around me. Even when I cry out, 'Violence!' I am not answered; I call aloud, but there is no justice" (Job 19:6–7). Only after Job has poured out his anger and anguish, it seems, can he say, "For I know that my Redeemer lives, and that at the last he will stand upon the earth" (Job 19:25). In other words, it may take a great deal of pastoral care and patient spiritual direction for some people to come to the point of trusting life and the Author of life enough to let the desire for "I know not what" into their consciousness.

Job's "friends" tried to derail him from expressing his desires to God. In his misery, he wants God to speak to him. Job will not lie and say, as his friends insinuate, that he deserves his calamities because of his sins. He will not accept the "just-world hypothesis" proposed by his friends, according to which a person's sufferings must be deserved. No, he knows that he does not deserve the awful fate that has befallen him, and he desires to speak directly to God and to hear God's answer. Often enough, we Christians are like Job's friends. To a mother who has just lost her only child, we might say, "God knows best," and thus make it difficult for her to voice her outrage at God and her need for God's own answer to this awful loss.

Sometimes we feel that we have to defend God against the anger directed at God by suffering people. Yet the anger may be the most authentic way for a person to relate to God and to express a desire to know God's response.

Finally, in chapters 38 through 41 of the book of Job, God does answer out of the whirlwind. The response may not sound very comforting or apologetic to us, but apparently Job was satisfied, for he said, "I had heard of you by the hearing of the ear, but now my eye sees you; therefore I despise myself, and repent in dust and ashes" (Job 42:5–6). Moreover, God then speaks to Job's friends. "My wrath is kindled against you and against your two friends; for you have not spoken of me what is right, as my servant Job has" (Job 42:7). Whatever else God's speech from the whirlwind might mean, it certainly does not mean that Job has lost God's friendship by so strongly voicing his desire to have God answer him.

Another biblical instance of an attempt to derail a desire directed toward God comes in the first chapter of the first book of Samuel. Hannah, one of the two wives of Elkanah, is barren and miserable. She wants a son. Her husband, Elkanah, seeing her weeping and fasting, says to her, "Hannah, why do you weep? Why do you not eat? Why is your heart sad? Am I not more to you than ten sons?" (1 Samuel 1:8). In other words, Elkanah wants Hannah to forget her desire and be satisfied with what she has. In the story, we do not hear Hannah's reply, but her actions tell us that she was not satisfied with Elkanah's entreaties. She went to the temple. "She was deeply distressed and prayed to the Lord, and wept bitterly" (1 Samuel 1:10). Indeed, when accused of being drunk by Eli, the priest, she says, "No, my lord, I am a woman deeply troubled . . . I have been pouring out my soul before the Lord" (1 Samuel 1:15). Hannah knows what she wants, and she is not afraid to tell God over and over what it is.

Often we tell ourselves, or we are told, in an effort to quell our desires, to look at all the good we already have. We can be made to feel guilty and ungrateful for desiring what we want, but if we do suppress our desires without being satisfied that God has heard us, then, in effect, we pull back from honesty with God. Often, the result for our relationship with God is polite distance or cool civility. Perhaps God cannot or will not grant what we want, but for the sake of the continued development of the relationship, we need to keep letting God know our real desires until we are satisfied or have heard or felt some response. In 2 Corinthians, Paul says, "a thorn was given me in the flesh, a messenger of Satan to torment me. . . . Three times I appealed to the Lord about this, that it would leave me, but he said to me, 'My grace is sufficient for you, for power is made perfect in weakness'" (2 Corinthians 12:7–9). Paul could now stop making his desire known because he knew God's answer.

> So, I will boast all the more gladly of my weaknesses, so that the power of Christ may dwell in me. Therefore I am content with weaknesses, insults, hardships, persecutions, and calamities for the sake of Christ; for whenever I am weak, then I am strong. (2 Corinthians 12:9–10)

Such a conviction does not come from theological or spiritual nostrums, but from the experience of growing transparency between Paul and the Lord.

Too often we use the hard-won wisdom of someone like Paul to short-circuit a similar transparency in our own relationship with the Lord. A woman may, for example, be experiencing the "dark night of the soul" and not like it at all. Her desire may be for it to be removed. She may be helped by the knowledge that others before her have experienced the same thing and have been the better for it, but such knowledge does not have to satisfy her desire to be rid of the dark night. A short circuit in the relationship might occur if she tells herself or is told by her spiritual director to squelch her desire "because the experience is good for you." What she needs to experience is God's response, not a theorem of spiritual theology. She needs to know (really, not notionally) that God does want this darkness for the good of their relationship. Such real knowledge comes only through mutual transparency.

Most of the healing miracles of the New Testament depend on the desire of the recipient for healing. The example of the blind beggar Bartimaeus (Mark 10:46–52) stands out, but it is not unusual. "When he heard that it was Jesus of Nazareth, he began to shout out and say, 'Jesus, Son of David, have mercy on me!' Many sternly ordered him to be quiet, but he cried out even more loudly, 'Son of David, have mercy on me!'" (Mark 10:47–48). Obviously, any number of voices trying to quiet Bartimaeus would not hinder him from expressing his desire.

These "voices" can come from within us as well as from without. "Jesus won't have time for the likes of me; other people have more important problems; things aren't so bad." These interior voices may be expressing our ambivalence about being healed. Just as Bartimaeus had made a way of life out of his blindness, we too may have made a way of life out of our own physical or psychological or spiritual limitations and may be afraid of what a future without them might be like. One person on a retreat thought he desired healing from a kind of darkness that seemed to rule his life. But then he heard the Lord ask, "Do you want me to heal you of this?" and he had to admit that he was not sure. He felt that God approved of the honesty of his response. The inner voices may also arise from our fear of expressing strong desires for healing only to have them dashed. "Suppose I really want to be healed and I hear the answer Paul got? What a disappointment!"[2] Desires are complex and often contradictory. However, once we have allowed the ambivalence and complexity of our desires to surface, we have something else to ask the Lord about.

In the Bartimaeus story, Jesus calls him over and asks, "What do you want me to do for you?" Bartimaeus is quite clear and unambivalent, "My teacher, let me see again." "Go," says Jesus, "*your faith* has made you well." I have emphasized Jesus' words. Without the faith of Bartimaeus, apparently, this miracle could not have occurred. The miracle requires a partnership between Jesus' healing power and desire to heal and Bartimaeus's faith and desire to be healed. Bartimaeus's faith is his desire in action.

An example may help to illustrate this point. Once, I was filled with anger and self-pity about the turn a friendship had taken and thought I was praying for healing. I was contemplating the story of the two blind men in Matthew 9:27–30. When I came to the part of the story where Jesus asks them, "Do you believe that I am able to do this?" I knew immediately that I was not ready to give up my self-pity and anger. If I did desire healing, it was with the same "but not yet" attitude with which Augustine at one time desired chastity. I did not have the faith found in the two blind men and in Bartimaeus, a faith that showed itself in unambivalent desire.

Another example that shows how desire is faith in action is provided by the story of the father of the boy with the evil spirit, reported in Mark 9:14–29. Instead of asking directly for a healing, the father says to Jesus, "but if you are able to do anything, have pity on us and help us." Because he did not believe in Jesus' power to heal, he could not desire the healing directly. Jesus says, "If you are able!—All things can be done for the one who believes," to which the father replies, "I believe; help my unbelief." In effect, the man is saying, "Help me to desire healing."

This last example brings us close to the nub of why desires are the raw material from which relationships are made. In order for the healing to occur, there must be a meshing of desires. Bartimaeus's desire for healing meets Jesus' desire to heal; without both desires there is no relationship, or at least no mutual relationship. This point is beautifully illustrated in the story of the leper.

> A leper came to him begging him, and kneeling he said to him, "If you choose, you can make me clean." Moved with pity, Jesus stretched out his hand and touched him, and said to him, "I do choose. Be made clean!" Immediately the leprosy left him, and he was made clean. (Mark 1:40–42)

Clearly desire meets desire. The kind of relationship Jesus desires is a mutual one, where desire meets desire.

The need for a partnership of desires becomes even clearer when we look at friendship. In John 15:15, Jesus says, "I have called you friends." He then indicates what that means as far as he is concerned: "because I have made known to you everything that I have heard from my Father." His desire has been to be fully transparent, to communicate to them all that he is. His desire meets their desire to know him as fully as possible. Of course, complete mutuality of friendship means that they desire to be fully transparent before him and that he desires to know them fully. Take away one side of these desires and there is no longer a mutual relationship.

On the apostles' part (and ours), the mere desire for mutual transparency does not carry it off. "Between the cup and the lip . . ." Our desires are ambivalent and complex; we are also fearful, and our fears get in the way of what we most deeply want. We need help and healing to grow toward mutual transparency with the Lord, and that help is available if we want it. If we notice, for example, that we want to know Jesus better but are afraid of the consequences, we can ask Jesus for help to overcome our fears. But again, we see that desire is the key to developing the relationship.

The retreatant who told God that he was not sure he wanted healing of the darkness that ruled his life provides another example of the reciprocity of relationships. Later in the same day, he became sure that he wanted healing and asked the Lord to heal him. The Lord's response was perplexing; "I can't," he seemed to say. He was enraged at such a response when he had overcome his own reluctance, and he let God know it in no uncertain terms. Yet still later in the day, he heard the Lord say, "But we can." He knew immediately that the Lord meant that he could live more out of joy than sadness if he kept desiring the Lord's helpful presence rather than withdrawing into himself. "We can" meant partnership.

At the beginning of this chapter, I stated that the real desires a person has are diagnostic of where the person is in terms of the Four Weeks of the Exercises. Let me now return to that point. If retreatants do not have a real trust in God's loving care and providence, they will not desire that God reveal their sinfulness to them. Without an experience-based belief in God's goodness and love, without, in other words, what I have earlier called an affective Principle and Foundation, people are too frightened of God to be able to say and mean the last words of Psalm 139: "Search me, O God, and know my heart; test me and know my thoughts. See if there is any wicked way in me, and lead me in the way everlasting" (Psalm 139:23–24). If there is no such real desire, then the First Week of the Exercises is not on. And at this point it seems that God's desire is not so much to reveal sinfulness as to convince the person that God is "Abba."

Similarly, if a person voices the desire to know Jesus in order to love him more and follow him more closely, yet in his prayer continually identifies with those who need healing, perhaps his real desire is to be healed. The desire of the Second Week to know Jesus shows itself in an interest in Jesus himself, in his values, his emotions, his dreams, his apostolate. If the person is not really interested in these matters, but *continually* focuses on his own needs and weaknesses, then the Second Week is not really in progress. Jesus himself may at this time more desire to heal than to call to companionship.

The difference between the First and Third Weeks also comes down to a difference in desire. In the First Week, the desire is to know that Jesus forgives us, that he died for our sins. The focus is on desiring to have a deep experience of how much Jesus loved us even though he knew how sinful we were. The desire of the Third Week is more to share in Jesus' passion insofar as this is possible. The focus is on what Jesus felt and suffered, and the desire is that he will reveal that to us. Retreat directors, I believe, do their most important work when they help their directees to discover what they really want. And so every retreat could begin with a contemplation of Jesus as he turns and says, "What are you looking for? What do you want?" (cf. John 1:38). As people hear these words and let them penetrate their hearts, they will come to know better what they desire; in other words, they will know better who they are at this time in their relationship with the Lord.

CHAPTER 3

Desire for God's Revelation

In this chapter, I want to demonstrate that the desires of the Spiritual Exercises are for God's personal revelation. People sometimes come to retreat with rather vaguely thought-out hopes and desires: "I want to get back to prayer"; "I need to recharge the spiritual batteries"; "I want to pray about a decision I have to make"; "I just want to be alone with God for a while." When the directors probe a bit into these desires, they regularly find that people want to experience the closeness and care of God but hold little hope that God will actually be a felt presence. In other words, some people expect too little of God and have an image of God as being more niggardly than God actually is.

This image of God may stem from a sense that God cannot be bothered with the "likes of me." It may stem from a sense that God is a distant and almighty figure. With such an image, whatever the source, people will not have those great desires that Ignatius hopes for in those who make the Exercises. They will not be able to enter the Exercises "with great spirit and generosity toward their Creator and Lord," as the Fifth Introductory Explanation puts it [n. 5]. Such people need a different picture of God. However, a new view of God is not attained from theological lectures or homiletic exhortations as much as from a different experience of God. Thus, a person with such an image of God is helped if she is guided to ask God for what she wants and needs; namely, an experience of God that will enable her to expect great things of God.

An example may help. A forty-year-old priest began a thirty-day retreat with a good deal of apprehension. He wanted to rekindle his devotion, but the prospect of praying four to five hours a day for thirty days was not a little daunting. The idea that God would speak intimately with him seemed foreign to him. He expected to "grunt his way through life" with God at a distance. At the same time, part of him wanted intimacy with God. In the first few days, he was surprised that the contemplation of natural beauty came easily to him and that the days did not drag. But he still could not believe that God would speak intimately with him. He did ask God to help him to believe this. About the fourth day, he was "surprised by joy," as it were. He had had an up-and-down day of prayer. When he woke up the next morning, he got into a conversation with God and felt that God was saying, "You are precious in my eyes." During the following few days, he see-sawed between believing in the experience and the possibilities it evoked and doubting its validity. Finally, about the eighth day, the reality of the experience and of other like experiences sank in. Here was an experience of God that he had secretly hoped for, but also did not expect. From then on he had great hopes and a great desire for God, only occasionally dampened by a return of his old image of self-in-relation-to-God. His image of God—and correlatively of himself—was changed by this prolonged experience.

A person may be a "house divided" as she begins the retreat. She may desire closeness to God, but she may also be afraid of God. She may fear that God will be terribly demanding. She may fear that God will come close as a condemning judge who frowns on her actions. Such a person needs help to put her ambivalent self before God. What she wants and needs is an experience of God that will overcome her fears. She might be encouraged to begin her prayer periods by asking God to reveal Godself in a way that will not frighten her away. Then she can do something that will give God a chance to respond to her desire. She may take a walk in a park or along the shore; she may quietly read Psalm 139. She wants a revelation of God that will help her to overcome her ambivalence.

Directors can help people to know God better by helping them know how God has been present in their lives up to the present moment, as we mentioned in chapter 1. The desire here is that God reveal to them their salvation history; namely, their history with God. A person asks God to reveal in detail how God has been present throughout his life. Then he recalls some person or place or incident from childhood and allows the memories to come freely. He tries not to control the thoughts, images, and memories, but to trust the process and the Spirit who dwells in our hearts to bring to mind what God wants to reveal at the present time. Some people fruitfully spend many days in such prayer and come to a new and different image of themselves in relation to God; that is, to a new revelation of God in relation to themselves.

Naturally, not every thought, memory, image, or revelation of who God has been for the person is equally important. But it is extraordinary how fruitful such prayer time is. It often allows the person to own, here and now, reactions, attitudes, and feelings that have been locked in the past. For instance, a man may cry for the first time for his father who died years before and may realize that one of the blocks to his intimacy with God is his inability to acknowledge his feelings of loss and anger. After a day or two of such prayer, most people are able to say with conviction, and sometimes for the first time, the words of Psalm 139: "For it was you who formed my inward parts; you knit me together in my mother's womb. I praise you, for I am fearfully and wonderfully made" (Psalm 139:13–14).

Once again, we recognize that the desire of the person is for a personal revelation of God, a revelation that will also disclose who he or she is before God. When such a desire is answered, then the person knows (in the Johannine sense that combines faith, knowledge, and love) that God is *his* or *her* God and that he or she is God's son or daughter. The person can affirm with inner conviction Ignatius's Principle and Foundation.

The Revelation of Sinfulness

Once people have had a rather deep experience of God's personal love and concern for them and have acknowledged the centrality of God in their lives and hearts, they often begin to think of examining their consciences. They become aware of how they have fallen short of God's hopes for them and for God's relationship with them. The director needs to help them to recognize their desires and to discern where they come from.

We have become so accustomed to seeing the examination of conscience as a thorough self-scrutiny that we forget the theological truism that only God can reveal sin to us. The sinner, precisely as sinner, is blind to his or her state. The conviction of sinfulness is a gift of God, an act of God's love. Thus, when the desire to examine sinfulness arises, it is important for the director to take time with the retreatant to clarify where the desire comes from. Examination of sins can become an exercise in self-absorption. It may even be a way of resisting the light of God's love and God's view of one's sinfulness. The clearest example of such resistance is the self-scrutiny of the scrupulous person. What such self-scrutiny unconsciously but effectively blocks out is God's revelation of love for the person and of the scrupulous person's real sinfulness; namely, his or her unwillingness or inability to accept that love. Concern for "my sins" may effectively keep the light of God's scrutiny from illuminating the need for conversion.

If people have come to a deep trust of God's love and concern, they may spontaneously ask God to reveal any wayward ways, or they may be encouraged to do so by the director. They make their own the words of Psalm 139: "Search me, O God, and know my heart; test me and know my thoughts. See if there is any wicked way in me, and lead me in the way everlasting" (Psalm 139:23–24). God is being asked to reveal God's ways, to root out all that hinders intimacy and discipleship. When the prayer begins this way, the person often is surprised to find that sins expected to be on the docket are not even brought to mind, while something else is revealed and becomes the focal point for conversion, such as an attitude of self-righteousness or an unwillingness to receive. God has been allowed to reveal God's own view of the relationship, and that view turns out to be different than expected.

People often discover that their sinfulness is not so much in their acts of commission or omission as in their unwillingness to be open and honest with

God about these acts. They find out that God wants intimacy with them, warts and all, and that they have been preventing that intimacy by being unwilling or unable to speak the whole truth to God. Their sin, in other words, consists at least partly in not believing that God will forgive them and that God does indeed love sinners. They also find out that their unwillingness to be open with God stems from their reluctance to look honestly at their lives in God's presence. The revelation of sinfulness reveals who we are, but it also reveals who God is and who he wants to be for us.

Even when people have experienced the forgiving love of God, they may have difficulty facing, in its stark reality, the fact that Jesus died for them, knowing they were sinners. That he died for all human beings is accepted and affirmed, but the sticking point is the very personal experience that "he died for *me* in the full knowledge of who I am." People want to believe this truth, but they can also be afraid, sometimes even terrified, of approaching the crucified Jesus in their imagination and looking him in the eyes.

Whatever the source of these fears—whether they arise from the reluctance to accept such love, from the apprehension that Jesus will not be looking at us with love, or from the fear of the demands such love will make—they are real enough, and the prayer can be very difficult. The director would do best not to argue with retreatants, but to help them to ask Jesus to reveal himself in such a way that they can accept such love. They are encouraged to share their fears with him and to approach him as best they can. It may take days, but they should not skip this process and move on, because this point is crucial for their subsequent relationship with God and with Jesus. If this stumbling block is removed by the grace of God, then they will experience at a profound level the free and freeing love of God for them precisely as who they are. They will know that they are loved sinners, and they will also know that God really is a lover of sinners.

The Desire to Know Jesus

The desire of the Second Week, "to ask for an interior knowledge of Our Lord, who became human for me, that I may love him more intensely and follow him more closely" [n. 104], is obviously a desire for revelation. We can only know Jesus intimately if he reveals himself. We ask for this grace and then contemplate the Gospel stories, not in order to understand the Gospels better, but because by contemplating these privileged writings, we give the living Lord Jesus a chance to reveal himself. We want Jesus to reveal to us his values, his loves and hates, his dreams and hopes, and especially his hopes for our relationship with him and for our lives.

As Jesus becomes more and more real, people may find him more challenging and daunting than they had expected him to be. He may show himself as having desires for them that they resist. He may desire that they give up everything and follow him in apostolic discipleship. They may recognize that they can freely respond yes or no and that they will not jeopardize his love for them by saying no. They, too, develop new or different desires toward him; they may desire to be chosen for apostolic discipleship, realizing that Jesus is free to choose them or not. The experience of many people in this Week, in other words, is of developing an adult relationship with the living Lord Jesus.

A desire for a more intimate revelation of Jesus is the way many people express the grace of the Third Week. They have come to a personal knowledge and a deep love of Jesus, and they now ask that he share his suffering self with them, that he let them share in his experience of the suffering and death that made him who he now is. It is important for directors to point out that they are asking for a grace, something that is not in their own power to attain. Many think that they can easily enter the contemplation of the passion and death of Jesus, only to find that their prayer is dry and difficult. One cannot enter into another's sufferings unless the other reveals him- or herself. Retreatants need to ask Jesus to reveal himself so that they can be sorrowful and compassionate with him. When he begins to reveal himself, they may well find that they have asked for more than they expected, and they may strongly resist letting this revelation penetrate their hearts. The Third Week very often is a struggle.

The desire that Jesus reveal his triumph, his joy, and the experience of having come through to resurrection, and the desire to rejoice with him, is the grace of the Fourth Week. Here again the director stresses that the person is asking for a grace or a revelation. The Fourth Week experience is not automatic, a climax that can be experienced just by contemplating the Resurrection narratives. Jesus must reveal himself. Moreover, they may well resist this knowledge of Jesus just as they have resisted earlier self-knowledge. Resurrection, for example, does not mean sweet revenge on one's enemies. The triumph may not be as one had expected. Once again, we find that the desire for revelation is an ambivalent one because God and God's Son are a surprising mystery.

Conclusion

When directors and retreatants look at the graces asked for in retreat as requests for revelation, perspectives change. For one thing, people realize more clearly that prayer is a matter of relationship. Intimacy is the basic issue, not answers to problems or resolutions "to be better." Many of life's problems and challenges have no answers; we can only live with and through them. Problems and challenges, however, can be faced and lived through with more peace and resilience if people know that they are not alone. A man's wife will not return from the dead, but the pain is more bearable when he has poured out his sorrow, his anger, and his despair to God and has experienced God's intimate presence. Second, people recognize more clearly that willpower alone cannot help them achieve "success" in prayer. It is much clearer that what one desires is a gift that only God can supply.

Freedom is at the heart of the process. No one can coerce personal revelation or intimacy. God cannot be forced and neither can the retreatant. There are some graces that God has freely decided to give to everyone who will accept them. God wants to save and liberate all of us; God loves us all to the point of letting Jesus die for us, and God wants us to accept that love. But the call to apostolic discipleship has not been promised to everyone who has asked for it. And certain desires, such as to be let into the suffering heart of Jesus, are not granted or are only granted after a long time of waiting. On the other hand, we need to recognize much more clearly that freedom also means that we are free before God. Directors should not try to coerce people to ask for what they do not yet want or are too ambivalent to desire honestly. God seems to want spontaneous love, not dumb submission.

The relationship with God and with Jesus tends to take on a more adult flavor when people begin to look at prayer in this interpersonal way. They realize that they are not asking for graces, much as a child might ask for candy, but for intimacy. While they wisely approach such an enterprise with fear and trembling, they nonetheless can do so as adults who know that intimacy requires maturity on their part.

CHAPTER 4

The Principle and Foundation

As it stands in the Spiritual Exercises, the Principle and Foundation is a rather dry theological statement of the reality of the human situation. People often fail to recognize that this set of truths is based not so much on deductions from theological premises as on reflection on lived experience in the light of theology. In a monograph, Joseph Tetlow convincingly shows that Ignatius's text is based on the experience of our continuing creation. He maintains that this experience is

> that we are being created momently by our God and Lord in all concrete particulars and that we are listening to God's summons into life when we let ourselves hear our most authentic desires, which rise out of God's passionate, creative love for us.[1]

Since Ignatius's text and Tetlow's interpretation express a universal, everyone must be able to have an experience that draws him or her to the knowledge, love, and service of God. Can we point to an experience that seems universal and that could thus ground these statements?[2]

In *Let This Mind Be in You,* Sebastian Moore suggests that we all have experiences of desiring "I know not what," experiences that are also accompanied by a feeling of great well-being. These are experiences, he says, of being touched by the creative desire of the God who desires us into being and continues to hold us in being. "God could," he says, "be defined—or rather pointed to—by this experience, as that which . . . causes in us that desire for we know not what which is the foundational religious experience."[3] He refers to the autobiography of C. S. Lewis, in which Lewis describes such an experience:

> As I stood before a flowering currant bush on a summer day there suddenly arose in me without warning, and as if from a depth not of years but of centuries, the memory of that earlier morning at the Old House when my brother had brought his toy garden into the nursery. It is difficult to find words strong enough for the sensation which came over me; Milton's "enormous bliss" of Eden . . . comes somewhere near it. It was a

sensation, of course, of desire; but desire for what? Not, certainly, for a biscuit tin filled with moss, nor even (though that came into it) for my own past . . . and before I knew what I desired, the desire itself was gone, the whole glimpse withdrawn, the world turned commonplace again, or only stirred by a longing for the longing that had just ceased. It had taken only a moment of time; and in a certain sense everything else that had ever happened to me was insignificant in comparison.[4]

Only later in life did Lewis discover that what he desired was the Mystery we call God.

In *The Sacred Journey,* Frederick Buechner provides a wonderful example from his own life, an example that also illustrates how multidimensional such experiences are. After his father's tragic suicide, his mother took him and his brother to Bermuda. Near the end of their stay, the thirteen-year-old Buechner was sitting on a wall with a girl who was also thirteen, watching ferries come and go. Quite innocently, he says,

our bare knees happened to touch for a moment, and in that moment I was filled with such a sweet panic and anguish for I had no idea what that I knew my life could never be complete until I found it. . . . It was the upward-reaching and fathomlessly hungering, heart-breaking love for the beauty of the world at its

most beautiful, and, beyond that, for that beauty east of
the sun and west of the moon which is past the reach
of all but our most desperate desiring and is finally the
beauty of Beauty itself, of Being itself and what lies at
the heart of Being.[5]

Buechner himself acknowledges that there are many
ways of explaining this experience. However, he goes
on, "looking back at those distant years I choose not
to deny, either, the compelling sense of an unseen
giver and a series of hidden gifts as not only another
part of their reality, but the deepest part of all."[6]

Anne Tyler's novel *Dinner at the Homesick Restaurant*
provides an example of this experience happening to an
ordinary person. Pearl Tull is a blind old dying woman
who was abandoned by her husband and thus brought
up three children alone. She lives with one of her sons,
Ezra, and his task each day is to read to her some of her
childhood diary. Most of the entries are quite banal, and
Pearl quickly has him move on. Just before she dies,
Ezra riffles through some entries and begins to read.

"Early this morning," he read to his mother, "I went out
behind the house to weed. Was kneeling in the dirt by
the stable with my pinafore a mess and perspiration
rolling down my back, wiped my face on my sleeve,
reached for the trowel, and all at once thought, Why I
believe that at just this moment I am absolutely happy."

His mother stopped rocking and grew still.

"The Bedloe girl's piano scales were floating out her window," he read, "and a bottle fly was buzzing in the grass, and I saw that I was kneeling on such a beautiful green little plant. I don't care what else might come about, I have had this moment. It belongs to me."

That was the end of the entry. He fell silent.

"Thank you, Ezra," his mother said. "There's no need to read any more."[7]

Obviously Pearl wanted to remember that foundational experience once more before she died; perhaps, too, she wanted Ezra to know that she had had it.

Not everyone who has such experiences interprets them as Frederick Buechner did, as experiences of God. C. S. Lewis, for example, did not do so until much later in life. But a believer can interpret such experiences in this way and can also draw out their implications. Notice that the experiences speak of desire for "I know not what." In another book, Lewis describes the joy he experienced as "an intense longing" that, though intense and even painful, is somehow a delight, indeed a greater delight than the fulfillment of any other desire.[8] Moreover, the experience includes a sense of great well-being. While in the experience, we do not worry about ourselves, our worth, or our goodness, but rather we seem to take for granted our being in the world. Sebastian Moore interprets the experience, quite rightly, as an experience of being desired into existence by God. Hence, we are desirable.

The most significant aspect of these experiences, however, is that they happen in the present, not at some moment of creation in the past. Our image of the creation of the universe refers to something that happened long ago, at the moment of the big bang or whatever means God used to set the creative process in motion. When we imagine God creating us, we tend to think of our creation as happening when we were conceived or born. But the experiences we have been discussing are described as happening to people who are already alive. If these are experiences of the creative touch of God, then we are talking about an action of God that is going on continually, not one that happened in some distant point in time. When we have such experiences, we are experiencing the present action of God.

How are we to understand such an assertion? The late Scottish philosopher John Macmurray developed a philosophy of the person based on the primacy of action over thought.[9] Action includes thought because any action is intended. When I act, I know what I intend to do. Events are different from actions in that events are not intended; they just happen. Actions include events. Let me give an example of an action, as Macmurray understands the term. This book is one action of mine because it is governed by one intention. I want to present my approach to the Exercises in such a way that it will have an influence on the book's readers. This one action includes many other actions, such as the many actions of rewriting it, and many events, such as the typing skills that occur without my intention. Because my intention is to have an influence on my readers, my one action also depends on my audience and their willingness to pay attention to the book. Thus this printed book is my one action. In reading and reflecting on this book, the reader is also encountering me. In an analogous way, we can understand the universe as one action of God. Hence, God is always active, always doing God's thing, as it were. At every moment of the existence of the universe, God is creating this world and everything in it, and we are encountering God whether we are aware of it or not.

If the universe is one action of God, then God has one intention in creating it. What does God intend with this one action, which is the universe? We only know the intentions of persons (and only persons can perform actions) if they reveal them to us. If someone does not reveal to me the intention of his action in my regard, I may infer that he intended to help me, but I might be wrong. He may have just acted inadvertently. I can only *know* his intention if he reveals it to me truthfully. If this is true of human beings, how much more true is it of God? Has God revealed to us God's intention in creating the universe? Christians believe that God has done so in the person of Jesus the Christ.

The kingdom of God that Jesus preached can be seen as the intention of God in creating the universe. God, it seems, creates this universe to invite all persons to share the interpersonal life of the Trinity. Moreover, this intention has implications for our present age; the kingdom of God is both of this world and not of this world. God wants all persons to live as sisters and brothers of Jesus and in harmony with the whole created universe; hence, God has a stake in how each of us lives our lives. Tetlow, in his monograph, speaks not so much of the kingdom of God as of "God's project," which seems to come down to the same thing. God's project

> suggests . . . a finite reality that exists in God but that is not God. A project is a concrete event, an ongoing activity that requires improvisation and adjustment. . . . To God's project, all things great and small are required to

make a contribution out of the self, and indeed will make a contribution whether by choice or not, whether embracing God's hopes or attempting to frustrate them.[10]

Thus, when we have foundational experiences such as those I described earlier, we are experiencing the creative action of God, who is always working to bring us and all persons under the reign or kingdom of God, into the inner life of the Trinity. We may not draw out all the implications of such experiences, but nonetheless, I believe that we can do so. In fact, Ignatius has drawn out these implications from his own experiences and has distilled them, albeit in a language colored by his own age and theology, in the Principle and Foundation. This is the point of Tetlow's monograph. When we experience the desire for "I know not what," we are experiencing God's one creative action, which calls each one of us and the whole universe into being with the intention of drawing all persons into the one community, the Trinity. No wonder C. S. Lewis could say that he was "surprised by Joy," by a desire that "had taken only a moment of time" but that made "everything else that had ever happened to me . . . insignificant in comparison."

When I have the experience of desiring "I know not what," I am experiencing God as creating me *now* in all the particulars of my present existence. While in thrall to that experience, I do not worry about my past failures and sins or about what the future might hold. I feel at one with the universe and as whole as I could possibly be. Moreover, the desire I experience is the deepest desire within me. That desire is in tune with God's one intention in creating the universe, and that desire can become the ruling passion of my life if I let it. When we experience this desire, it is God's Holy Spirit drawing us into the community that is the Trinity. While we are in the power of this desire, everything else becomes relative before the absolute Mystery we desire. Moreover, insofar as this desire reigns in our hearts, we desire to live out our lives in harmony with this desire and want to do whatever will more readily bring us to the object of our desire. Hence, we want to live in harmony with God's creative purpose in creating us, to choose what will be more in tune with our desire for union with God. Ignatius spells out the implications of the foundational experience of God's creative touch in the Principle and Foundation.

Because God is God and because our ultimate happiness lies in living in harmony with God's intention for the universe and for each one of us, Ignatius calls upon us to be "indifferent" to all created things. In his recent translation, Ganss notes that the term is a key technical term in Ignatian spirituality. However, "in no way does it mean unconcerned or unimportant. It implies interior freedom from disordered inclinations."[11] In the monograph already cited, Tetlow translates the word Ignatius uses, which Ganss has translated as "indifferent," as "at balance," which comes much closer to Ignatius's intent. Caught in the pull of the desire for "I know not what," we do not want anything to block the fulfillment of that desire. Thus, before every choice we make we want to be at balance in order to discern or discover what will more surely bring us what we most deeply desire.

Roger Haight makes the point that "the symbol of the kingdom of God can mediate the experience that as personal and as creator God has a will and intention for creation and that, as a creature, the self participates in that intention."[12] Later, he notes the transforming power of this symbol.

> The special note of the kingdom of God is that the one encountered, God, is encountered as having a divine intention for the world and human history. The symbol thus appeals more directly to human will and influences more pointedly human action. An appreciation of its transcendent meaning fairly demands a conversion to a desire to be in conformity with God's will. The

symbol thus transforms natural ethics into an expression of God's will. It transforms a person's responses to the world into simultaneous responses to God. It transforms goals and ideals into the goals and ideals of God. It can thus have an impact on the transformation of the world. The kingdom of God is of this world and transcendently more than that.[13]

The person who takes the foundational experience seriously will want to make the full Spiritual Exercises so that he or she can be freed from any hindrances to choosing what is more in tune with what God wants and discerning better what that is.

Conclusion

In this chapter, we have been reflecting on the Principle and Foundation and on the experiences upon which it is based. Ignatius's text is not derived from theological premises, although theological premises and principles are at work in the elaboration of the written exercise. The experience that underlies it seems to be an experience of God creating this universe and everything in it with the intention of drawing all persons into the inner life of the Trinity and into harmonious relations with one another and with the whole universe. Because God is the One Creator, this experience is available to all people according to their capacity. However, even those who have vivid and awesome experiences of this creative touch of God may not, and often do not want to, pay enough attention to the experiences to draw out their implications for their lives.

For those who do pay attention and want to draw out the implications of their experience of the Mystery, who calls everything and "me" into being for a purpose, Ignatius offers the Spiritual Exercises as a powerful means "to overcome oneself, and to order one's life, without reaching a decision through some disordered affection" [n. 21]. Because such people experience, in an overpowering way, what God intends with the universe, with every person and with "me," they recognize the deep disorder of our world and of human beings and of "myself," and they beg God to convert them and all human beings.

Moreover, in our day, because we are so aware of the interdependence of everything in the universe, the experience of God's creative action brings us to recognize how many of the institutions and social structures that influence our lives are contrary to God's intention, and we beg God to give us the courage and the willingness to do our part to change these unjust institutions and structures.

CHAPTER 5

Transition Points in the Dynamic of the Exercises

In this chapter, I want to look at the transition points in the dynamic of the Spiritual Exercises. That is, I want to indicate the kinds of experiences I look for in a person that demonstrate a readiness to begin a particular set of exercises, or Week. The Spiritual Exercises are not a drill that one goes through without any regard to what one is experiencing. The director's main task, after listening, is to help the directee to know what he or she authentically desires. These desires can be seen as touchstones to determine how ready the person is to move on to a new stage of the Exercises.

The Principle and Foundation

As we noted in the last chapter, the Principle and Foundation is the fruit of both Ignatius's experience and his later study of theology. Ignatius, after much spiritual agony, came to experience God as the deepest desire of his heart; he realized that he was created for God and that nothing else would satisfy him. Moreover, through his experiences at Manresa, he came to have a felt knowledge of God's purpose for the creation of the universe. In the Principle and Foundation, he distilled the fruit of those experiences in the light of his later theological studies.

Through mystical experience, Ignatius came to believe that the perfect community, the Trinity, which is motivated purely by love, creates a universe in which persons made in the image of God are continually being drawn by the cords of divine love into the inner life of the Trinity. In the depths of our hearts, we are being drawn by a desire for union with God and thus with all other persons. Ignatius came to believe that the Trinity wants each of us to live our lives in such a way as to be part of the dream of God, collaborators with God in bringing about the kingdom. We cannot, therefore, ultimately be happy and at peace in this life unless our lives are in tune with God's dream for the universe and for each one of us.

If we have this experience of God as the Creator who loves us into existence for community with God, then we will have a positive spiritual identity; we will know that we are beloved of God, the apple of God's eye. I have called this experience the affective Principle and Foundation needed to make the Spiritual Exercises. With this experience firmly established in our hearts, we will, at least inchoately, realize that we should not let anything get in the way of our attaining the end God has in mind for us. We will want to beg God to remove from us all inordinate attachments (which Gerald May calls addictions[1]), and this will make us ready to begin the Spiritual Exercises.

I suspect that many of us know from our own and others' experience that it is often difficult to let this experience of God's dream and creative love for us take root in our hearts. A poor self-image can get in the way, as can an image of God as one who is "always snooping around after sinners."[2] Scrupulous people, for example, have the devil's own time coming to believe that God loves them, warts and all. It took four years of careful spiritual direction by Ignatius before Pierre Favre, who later became one of the best directors of the Exercises, was ready to make the retreat. Ignatius himself was so plagued by scruples that, he tells us, he came close to suicide.[3] Only after a long time of siege by such scruples did he come to believe that God was not a tyrant. We will only ask God to purify us of our inordinate attachments and to reveal to us our sins and sinful tendencies when we believe in our bones that God is on our side and has our good at heart.

If what I have just noted has any validity, then we need to be patient with ourselves and with those to whom we minister. We have to be willing to take the time and to use our ingenuity to help ourselves and others to have, and to have confidence in, such experiences of a loving, creative God who invites us into community with the Trinity. These experiences are the firm foundation upon which a developing relationship with God is built.

Before this foundation is firmly built, people live in an illusory world. They believe that God needs to be placated, and yet that God is really implacable. They try, as Paul did, to fulfill the letter of every law in order to deserve, if not the love of God, then at least God's grudging acceptance. The illusion comes down to the belief that "I am rotten to the core and unlovable," and many people live in this illusory world. Those who minister in the church need to develop the spiritual techniques or pastoral practices that will help people to overcome this illusion and to come to a basic trust in God. Only with such a grasp of reality will they (and we) be able to enter the First Week of the Exercises, which requires the authentic desire in people to have God reveal to them how they and the world have fallen short of God's dream for them and the world.

The First Week

When people are becoming firmly grounded in the experience of God as a loving Creator, as the Abba (dear Father) of Jesus, they often experience a sort of honeymoon period in prayer. They relish spending time relating to God, and prayer seems easy and delightful. But the honeymoon period cannot last forever. We all know that we have fallen short of the glory of God, and we become aware of our resistances to further closeness to God. We want God to remove these barriers, but at the same time we are afraid of what such a removal will entail. We come to recognize that the world is not at all the Garden of Eden that God intended. God has begun to reveal to us our own and our society's sins and sinful tendencies. We are entering the dynamic of the First Week of the

Spiritual Exercises, in which our desire is that God reveal to us our own and our world's sinfulness and that he forgive us and enable us to live more and more in the freedom of the children of God.

As we have seen, the movements of the Spiritual Exercises are driven by the desire stated in the second or third prelude that Ignatius puts before every meditation or contemplation. These desires cannot be forced; they must be authentic desires of our hearts. If we do not have the desire Ignatius expects to drive the dynamic of the First Week, for example, the only thing we can do is ask God to give us the desire. One of the key questions we can put to ourselves for our own prayer as well as to those we direct is "What do I really want right now from God or in my relationship with God?" Honesty about our real desires is crucial for growth in our relationship with God and, indeed, in any relationship. In giving the Exercises to groups of people, we need to keep in mind that the people in the group will vary widely in their desires. As we give points for prayer, it would be good to remind our listeners to move with their own authentic desires.

In the First Week of the Exercises, then, our desire is for God to reveal how far short we have fallen of God's dream for us and how our inordinate attachments (addictions) keep us from living out God's dream. But we also want to know that God still loves us, warts and all; we want to know that we are loved sinners. Only such knowledge will give us the grace and the impetus to try to overcome our sinful tendencies. Moreover, we want God to reveal to us how far short our society, our culture, our church, and our world have fallen of God's dream without losing God's loving care.

The fact that we need reassurance about God's love of us sinners indicates that at this stage of our spiritual journey we also labor under an illusion. It is difficult for us to believe in our bones that God loves sinners. Yet Jesus died for us *sinners*. This illusion, like the one that says, "I am rotten to the core and totally unlovable," also dies hard, yet only with its death and burial can we be free. While we live with this illusion, we continually try to prove that we are lovable; we continually try to save ourselves. We must let Jesus wash our feet when our sinfulness is out in the open; we must look into the eyes of Jesus dying on the cross for our sins and there see love. Only then are we living in the real world, which is still, in spite of all its crookedness, a world where God continues to draw us into community with the Trinity, where Jesus gave up his life precisely for us as sinners.

When we are freed from this illusion, we know in the depths of our hearts that

> God so loved the world that he gave his only Son, so that everyone who believes in him may not perish but may have eternal life. Indeed, God did not send the Son into the world to condemn the world, but in order that the world might be saved through him. (John 3:16–17)

With this deep heartfelt knowledge we can speak to Jesus on the cross as a friend speaks to a friend. Then we will be able to ask ourselves, motivated by genuine love and shame rather than by unhealthy feelings of guilt, "What have I done for Christ? What am I doing for Christ? What ought I to do for Christ?" Now, perhaps, we are ready to allow the desire to know, love, and follow Christ to rise in our hearts.

The Second Week

The desire of the Second Week of the Exercises is expressed in the third prelude Ignatius suggests before each contemplation. "Here it will be to ask for an interior knowledge of Our Lord, who became human for me, that I may love him more intensely and follow him more closely" [n. 104]. A fundamental

shift in orientation has occurred in those who have
this desire. Prior to this shift, the focus has been on
us and our needs. We have wanted to know in a
heartfelt way that God is where we are, with us in our
brokenness, our sinfulness, our desperate need. With
this shift in desire, we now want to be where Jesus is;
we want to know him and his values and his mission,
and we want to be part of that mission.[4] The difference
might be illustrated by two different images of ourselves
in relation to Jesus. In the First Week, we are like the
blind man Bartimaeus, who wants Jesus to give him
succor and heal his blindness. In the Second Week,
we are like the now seeing Bartimaeus, who follows
Jesus "on the way" (Mark 10:52).

Ignatius did not believe that many people were
ready for this shift of perspective. Hence he was
slow, it seems, to give the full Exercises. There are
many who, because of the physical or psychological
traumata they have suffered in life, find it almost
impossible to focus for long on anything but their
own need for healing. I will use the man from whom
the legion of demons was driven out as an example.
After the legion was driven out, "the man who had
been possessed by demons begged him that he
might be with him. But Jesus refused, and said to
him, 'Go home to your friends, and tell them how

much the Lord has done for you, and what mercy he has shown you'" (Mark 5:18–19). I realize that I am reading into the text, but perhaps, we could say, he was too scarred by what he had suffered to be able to take on the rigors that radical discipleship with Jesus entails. At any rate, we might keep in mind the possibility that people can only be hurt by being pushed into a desire to follow Jesus that is beyond their capacities.

Those who desire to know Jesus in order to love him more and follow him more closely will also encounter resistance to the call of Jesus. They will be as blind as the disciples, who after each of the three predictions of the Passion showed how completely they had missed the reality of the call. After all, those who follow Jesus too closely will suffer the same fate he suffered, or at least something similar. Here, the source of the resistance is much more realistic. The disciples, when they finally became like Christ, did suffer persecution and martyrdom.

Throughout the ages, those who have become like Christ through a close personal relationship have suffered as he suffered. Yet even here an illusion lies behind the resistance, the illusion that we can control our lives and our fate. We fear that if we surrender ourselves to the following of Christ, we will lose this control. This fear then keeps us from what we most desire at this stage of the spiritual journey; namely, closeness to Jesus. Throughout the Gospels, Jesus contrasts faith and fear and continually points out how useless fear is. In the final analysis, anyone who receives Jesus' call to discipleship hears these words of Jesus:

> If any want to become my followers, let them deny themselves and take up their cross and follow me. For those who want to save their life will lose it, and those who lose their life for my sake, and for the sake of the gospel, will save it. For what will it profit them to gain the whole world and forfeit their life? Indeed, what can they give in return for their life? (Mark 8:34–37)

Ignatius, of course, was an astute enough spiritual guide to know that we cannot follow Jesus in this way without the grace of God. In the meditation on the Two Standards, he indicates quite clearly that the two standards, or value systems, run right through each human heart. Hence, he proposes the triple colloquy in which we ask Mary, then Jesus, and then the Father to put us under the standard of Christ. We are addicted to possessions, to our reputations, and to our honor, and so we cannot, by ourselves, embrace the values of Christ, even though they are the real values that bring true happiness and peace in this life and in the next. In this sense, Christianity is what John Macmurray calls "real religion" in this remarkable statement from *Persons in Relation*:

> The maxim of illusory religion runs: "Fear not; trust in God and He will see that none of the things you fear will happen to you"; that of real religion, on the contrary, is "Fear not; the things that you are afraid of are quite likely to happen to you, but they are nothing to be afraid of."[5]

Ignatius suggests that those who want to be intimate followers of Jesus must beg over and over again to be freed from fears and illusory values in order to embrace the values of Jesus.

The Third Week

The desire of the Second Week of the Exercises is "for an interior knowledge of Our Lord, who became human for me, that I may love him more intensely and follow him more closely." We want to know his values, his loves, his hates, his dreams, his hopes. We want to know his heart so that we might be so much in love with him that nothing, not even our fear of suffering and death, will get in the way of our following him. As we are given the grace of the Second Week, we find ourselves more and more focused on Jesus and less and less on ourselves. Such a focus is not an achievement of our own will, but a gift of God for which we must continually beg. Indeed, the focus is not a once-and-for-all-time gift for most of us; our self-centeredness dies hard and may only be finally overcome in the grave. I wonder whether the difficult experience of overcoming self-centeredness led to the theological postulation of the existence of purgatory.

Nonetheless, those who do have the desire of the Second Week are gradually freed of enough of their self-centeredness to ask for the graces of the Two Standards and the Three Degrees of Humility. Jesus does become the love of their lives, their closest friend, their dearest companion. As they come to the end of this stage of their spiritual journey, they—like Bartimaeus after he receives his sight—want to follow Jesus on the way (Mark 10:52), the way of the cross. They are ready to begin the Third Week.

The desire of this Week, as Ignatius articulates it, is "to ask for sorrow, regret, and confusion, because the Lord is going to his Passion for my sins" [n. 193]. Once again, it is important to note that Ignatius is talking about a desire and that desires are not under our control. To desire to have compassion for Jesus, and to suffer with Jesus, is a gift of the love for Jesus that has grown in our hearts throughout the Second Week. Moreover, the presence of the desire does not preclude conflicting desires. Think of how difficult it is for very close friends or loved ones to share pain, suffering, and dying. We may want to suffer with our closest friend, but we also fear the consequences of that desire. To share his or her suffering cuts us to the quick. If he or she dies, we lose "half my soul," as Augustine described a dear one; no one easily accepts such a loss. In addition, our friend may not want to increase our pain by sharing what is really going on in him or her. Those who have worked with the terminally ill note that often both the dying person and her loved ones are terribly lonely precisely because of their mutual fears of "hurting one another," of "making it worse" for one another by sharing their real feelings.

In the case of Jesus, we presume that he wants to share his suffering with those who desire to suffer with him; we presume that he wants to give as much of himself to us as we want and can take (cf. the Contemplation to Attain Love, First Point, n. 234). The ambivalence lies in us. Moreover, we cannot presume that even a relatively deep experience of the Second Week of the Exercises will lead, during this retreat, to a deep desire to suffer with and have compassion for Jesus. What we can hope for is that during our continuing relationship with Jesus this desire will grow in us as a gift of his love for us. A very deep experience of the Third Week may only come many years after one has finished the full Spiritual Exercises.

Social psychologists speak of the "just-world hypothesis,"[6] which unconsciously guides much of our thoughts, feelings, and behavior. According to this hypothesis, suffering is deserved. Thus, if we hear that someone has cancer of the lungs, we presume that he has been a heavy smoker. If a mudslide wipes out a whole town, we wonder why the people built their town in that place. If a woman is raped, people have a tendency to presume that she went to the wrong part of town or made a poor choice of companion or got what she was asking for. We want to find a reason for a calamity. To understand this dynamic, we might reflect on our own reactions when we have heard some piece of bad news regarding ourselves. Behind the almost instinctive "Why me?" lies the just-world hypothesis, and the only answer that makes sense is that we must have done something wrong. If calamities are not somehow deserved, then we are all at risk at any moment, and that is a frightening prospect. This just-world hypothesis makes it difficult for any one of us to enter deeply into the suffering of another, no matter how close he or she is to us. In the case of Jesus, the just-world hypothesis is totally exploded. Here, the absolutely innocent one suffers horribly. This is another reason why it is difficult for us to desire wholeheartedly to suffer with and have compassion for Jesus.

Some of the more bizarre theological theories purporting to explain the suffering of Jesus might well stem from the unconscious sway of the just-world hypothesis. For instance, there is the theory that Jesus had to suffer so horribly in order to satisfy God's anger at the sins of humans, or that only the suffering of a human being who was God could make up for the infinite indignity suffered by God through sin. These theories, it seems to me, are concocted to explain why Jesus, the innocent one, had to suffer so horribly, thus safeguarding the just-world hypothesis. Yet anyone not beguiled by the hypothesis might ask how such theories square with Jesus' revelation of God as his "Abba," his "dear Father" (or "dear Mother"), and as overflowing love.

Thus we must expect that no matter how strong our desire to suffer with Jesus, there will be internal resistances to that desire. Death threatens us with annihilation, with the loss of all the relationships that make us who we are. In his Pulitzer Prize–winning book, *The Denial of Death,* Ernest Becker demonstrates quite well the pervasiveness of the fear of death in our culture and how desperately we strive to deny the possibility of death.[7] All the psychological defenses we put up to deny the reality of death will raise their heads as we approach the Third Week of the Spiritual Exercises.

Because of these resistances, Ignatius has us beg for what we desire over and over again. He knows from experience that one occasion of compassion for Jesus will not suffice to overcome the resistances. But in spite of the strength of the resistance, God's grace is not defeated.

> People do receive this gift of sorrow and compassion for Jesus, and they know that their sorrow is different from the sorrow they experienced in the First Week of the Exercises when they contemplated Jesus on the cross. Then they were sorry for their sins and marveled that in spite of the sins which had put Jesus on the cross he still looked on them with love. Now they are not focused on themselves much at all, but on Jesus and what he has gone through and is going through. One woman came in during a retreat with tears streaming down her face and said, "He's dead; I'm glad that his agony is over." And people who receive this grace of compassion for Jesus find that the compassion spills over to compassion for all the suffering people of this world. Indeed, they sense

that Jesus is still suffering in all the people who suffer, especially in those who are oppressed and ground down as he was. I think that such compassion for a suffering world means taking on the heart of Christ and the compassion of God. God, I believe, is revealing his own reactions to the horrors human beings perpetrate on one another and on God's beloved Jesus. The mystical body of Christ is experienced in a mysterious way when God gives us this gift of compassion for Jesus' suffering and the suffering of untold others.[8]

It may be that the deepest motivation to work for justice in our world arises from the compassion of the Third Week.

The Fourth Week

Ignatius expects that God will elicit a desire "for the grace to be glad and to rejoice intensely because of the great glory and joy of Christ our Lord" [n. 221] in those who have experienced some depth of compassion for Jesus. This shift in desire ushers in the Fourth Week of the Exercises. Notice that the person asks for a grace, something not in his own power to achieve. Secondly, notice that he asks to rejoice for Jesus' sake.

The fact that we ask for a grace in this Week indicates that the experience of joy in the resurrection of Jesus does not come automatically. Indeed, we do experience resistance to this grace, which seems strange. However, to experience this intense joy we have to be able to notice the wounds in Jesus' hands and feet. The Resurrection is not an undoing of the horrors of the Crucifixion. To experience the joy of Jesus we must be able to accept the mysterious "necessity" of such a horror. "Was it not necessary that the Messiah *should* suffer these things and then enter into his glory?" (Luke 24:26; italics mine). The only way that Jesus could be the glorified Jesus he now is (rather than some other Jesus without the marks of these particular wounds) was the way of the cross. This is the wisdom of Jesus.

It is very hard for us to come to this wisdom. In fact, on our own we cannot come to it—we need the grace of God. Hence, we must beg God for the ability to rejoice with Jesus, and rejoicing with him means accepting his cruel death. It was not just a bad dream, just as the pains and losses we suffer and will suffer in life are not just bad dreams. I also believe that we cannot fully rejoice in the life of our loved ones who have died and experience their risen life until we can accept their suffering and death. Not only does the fear of death keep us from fully enjoying our life; it also keeps us from rejoicing with the risen Jesus and with our loved ones who have joined him. I want to repeat once again Macmurray's maxim of real religion: "Fear not; the things that you are afraid of are quite likely to happen to you, but they are nothing to be afraid of."[9] The resurrection of Jesus shows real religion at its best. The Passion and death really did happen, but Jesus says they are nothing to be afraid of. When we receive the grace of rejoicing with Jesus in his glory, then we want to shout Alleluia over and over again.

Conclusion

In this chapter, I have tried to show some of the experiences and desires of people that indicate where they are in the dynamic progression of the Spiritual Exercises. Obviously, progress in the spiritual life is not a matter of smooth movement from one plateau to another. The experience of being a loved sinner is not a once-and-for-all achievement. The development of any relationship, and especially of the relationship with the Lord, is fraught with many peaks and valleys, with periods of strong development in intimacy and periods of regression to early stages of the relationship. Even a very deep experience of the full Spiritual Exercises, even one that culminates in a mystical experience of the Contemplation to Attain Love, does not preclude later regressions to earlier stages in one's relationship with the Lord. However, once we have experienced the heights of the relationship, we know how much God wants to give of Godself, and this knowledge sharpens the desire to return to that depth of relationship.

CHAPTER 6

Ignatian Contemplation: The Use of Imagination in Prayer

What was the original genial insight of Ignatius of Loyola? I would say that it was the idea that God can be found in all things, that every human experience has a religious dimension and religious meaning. The point is illustrated in the first chapter of the autobiography that Ignatius dictated to Gonçalves da Càmara. Ignatius, the fiery, brave, womanizing, ambitious knight, is convalescing at the castle of Loyola from the shattering of his leg by a cannonball. He tells us that he was much given to imagining himself as a knightly hero winning the favor of a great lady. He would spend hours in such daydreams.

Because, however, he could not get the romantic
novels he delighted in at Loyola Castle, he began to
look at the only reading matter on hand, a life of Christ
and a book of saints' lives. What he read also fed his
imagination, and he began to engage in daydreams of
outdoing the saints' austerities in following Christ.
Again these daydreams would last for hours. For a long
time, he did not notice any difference in his reactions
to these two sets of daydreams, yet the difference
was there. During the knightly daydreams, he felt
exhilarated, but after them he felt "dry and unhappy."
During the daydreams about imitating the saints, he
also felt exhilarated, but after these he "remained
happy and joyful." He then says:

> He did not consider nor did he stop to examine this
> difference until one day his eyes were partially opened
> and he began to wonder at this difference and to reflect
> upon it. From experience he knew that some thoughts
> left him sad while others made him happy, and little by
> little he came to perceive the different spirits that were
> moving him; one coming from the devil, the other
> coming from God.[1]

I believe that this little story depicts the emergence of
the core of Ignatian spirituality, that God can be found
in all things. If God can be discovered in daydreams,
then God can be found anywhere. In this chapter, I

want to reflect on the way God used Ignatius's imagination to lead him to conversion and on how the Exercises suggest the use of imagination in prayer.

Obviously, Ignatius had a strong imagination. He loved to read the romantic novels of his time, which fired his imagination and led him to dream of performing great exploits for his king, his country, and his "grande dame." He is not alone in his appreciation of romance and heroic tales. We can consider the popularity in the United States of the Western novel and movie, which have enkindled the imaginations of countless people and led them to consider themselves heroes or heroines bringing peace and justice to a harsh land. Or we can consider the popularity of J. R. R. Tolkien's trilogy, *The Lord of the Rings,* in which wizards, elves, dwarves, human beings, and hobbits (halflings) battle together to defeat the Dark Lord, who threatens doom to the world. I have read the trilogy five times, and each time tears come to my eyes when Frodo and the other hobbits are praised by the triumphant host for what they have accomplished to help defeat the Dark Lord. In the trilogy, Aragorn, the king, is almost the exact image of the king used by Ignatius in his kingdom meditation in the Exercises. He, too, shares all the toils and dangers of his men, leads them through the valley of the dead, and gives his all to save the world from the Dark Lord. Ignatius ate and drank such stories, and they fired his ambition, his desire to do great things.

God used this strong imagination to draw Ignatius to another kind of ambition. The Gospel stories and the lives of saints are imaginative literature too. They can fire the imagination, and in Ignatius's case, they did. We can imagine his distaste when these were the only books available at Loyola Castle. Gradually, however, they caught his interest, piqued his imagination, and the very same ambition that drove him to want to do great knightly deeds now caused him to imagine himself doing the same heroic deeds the saints did. In Christ, he found a king better than all imagined earthly kings. Finally, he noticed that the two sets of heroic imaginings had different repercussions in his heart.

Ignatius discovered that the Spirit of God was operative in both sets of imaginings: in the worldly imaginings, God's Spirit helped him to taste the ultimate vanity of such exploits, and in the images of following Christ, he helped him to taste the lasting joy of being with Christ. Actually, the way Ignatius uses the parable of the king to help fire up the imagination of the retreatant for the person of Jesus seems similar to the way the early Christians used the suffering servant stories of Isaiah to catch the imagination of their listeners. We can imagine them saying to one another: "Remember the story of the suffering servant in Isaiah? Well, in Jesus that story has come true, and in spades!"

Let me underline an important point here. Ignatius did not become a totally different person with this first discernment and his conversion. He was the same ambitious, driven man.[2] From his own experience, Ignatius learned how God could use his imaginative powers to teach him and draw him to a new way of life. We have already seen how the insight he gained from his daydreams during his convalescence was probably the kernel of the kingdom meditation that appears in the Spiritual Exercises before the contemplation of the public life of Jesus. Its purpose is to fire the imagination with desire to know Jesus better in order to love him more and follow him more closely. But Ignatius also learned that God uses the Gospel stories to draw us imaginatively into their world in order to reveal Godself to us. So let us look at some of the suggestions Ignatius makes in the Exercises.

In the contemplations of the Incarnation and the Nativity, Ignatius spells out suggestions that will apply for all the contemplations to come. In the

Second Prelude of all the contemplations of the life of Christ, Ignatius suggests "a composition, by imagining the place." In the contemplation of the Incarnation, he says, "Here it will be to see the great extent of the circuit of the world, with peoples so many and so diverse; and then to see in particular the house and rooms of Our Lady, in the city of Nazareth in the province of Galilee" [n. 103]. Immediately, we see that Ignatius goes well beyond the Gospel text in his suggestions for the imagination.

In the text of the contemplation itself, he fleshes out the panoramic view of the world to have us picture the Trinity "gazing on the whole face and circuit of the earth" [n. 106]. The imaginative breadth, the whole sweep of the earth under the gaze of God, is enormous, and then, in the manner of a modern zoom lens, the vision narrows to a tiny village in the backwater province of Galilee, and there to the home of a young girl. The three points that follow ask the person to "see the various persons, some here, some there," to "listen to what the persons on the face of the earth are saying," "what the Divine Persons are saying," and "what the angel and Our Lady are saying," and then to "consider what the people on the face of the earth are doing," "what the Divine Persons are doing," "what the angel and Our Lady are doing."

Nowhere in the Gospels is there any mention of what is going on in the rest of the world at the time of the Annunciation, nor is there mention of the counsels of the Holy Trinity. Yet Ignatius imagines what is behind the text. The Trinity must have taken counsel together, and for a reason. The reason, he imagines, is what they see in the world; namely, that people are going to hell and something needs to be done. Ignatius believes that if we let our imaginations go in this way, God will reveal to us who Jesus is and what he stands for so that we will fall in love with him and want to follow him.

The Nativity contemplation repeats the suggestion about the composition, imagining the place.

> Here it will be to see in imagination the road from Nazareth to Bethlehem. Consider its length and breadth, whether it is level or winds through valleys and hills. Similarly, look at the place or cave of the Nativity: How big is it, or small? How low or high? And how is it furnished? [n. 112]

Ignatius gives free rein to the imagination. Even though he had been to the Holy Land, he does not tell us how the terrain looks in reality. Each person is free to imagine what the terrain and place might look like. In the contemplation proper, he again advises the person to look at the people, to listen to what they are saying, and to consider what they are doing. He also adds a new person to the scene, a "maidservant," and suggests that "I will make myself a poor, little, and unworthy slave, gazing at them, contemplating them, and serving them in their needs, just as if I were there" [n. 114]. Such suggestions have freed people to imagine themselves in the scene in many ways. One pediatrician, for example, helped Mary to deliver Jesus and then held him in his arms and handed him to Mary. We can see that Ignatius expects that God will fulfill the desire of the person to get to know Jesus more intimately through the use of his or her imagination.

This is probably as good a place as any to discuss at more length the issue of imagination and fantasy in prayer. In the history of spirituality, there have been two main ways of prayer. One way stresses imageless, quiet prayer. In our day, this way is perhaps best exemplified by the use of centering prayer. One of the best-known teachers of this kind of prayer in the United States is the Cistercian monk Basil Pennington.[3] In Great Britain and many other English-speaking countries, the late Benedictine John Main had and continues to have a wide influence in this way of praying.[4] It is a helpful way of giving ourselves a chance to get in touch with the Mystery we call God at the center of our being.

The other way is exemplified by the Ignatian tradition and advocates using all of our faculties in prayer: sense, imagination, mind, and will. The stress on this way in this book should not be taken to mean that this way is normative for everyone. Both traditions have a venerable history, and I suspect that most people can find both ways helpful in meeting God. It could be that some kinds of personalities prefer one way, but I am not prepared to try to distinguish personality types and their affinities for prayer forms. I would encourage people to use whatever helps them to meet the living God. Methods are only means to that desired end. When the end is attained—that is, when God is encountered—then the relationship itself takes over.

But we need to say something about the use of imagination as a method that many have found very helpful for meeting God. We let the words of a Gospel scene touch our imaginations much as poetry or a novel might, asking the Lord to reveal himself to us in the process. We can imagine ourselves as actually a part of the scene, as Ignatius suggests.

At different times in our lives, we will find ourselves identifying more with one character than another in a Gospel scene. When, for example, we feel lost and unsure of our path, we may identify with Bartimaeus, the blind beggar of Mark 10, who cries out even against opposition, "Jesus, son of David, have mercy on me!" The opposition may be within us, in the inner voice that tries to tell us that prayer is futile. Then we too may have to cry out all the more, and we too may hear Jesus saying deep within us, "What do you want me to do for you?" And we can respond with our need to see. "My Teacher, let me see again; let me see my way." And then we can pour out our heart's pain to him.

At another time, we may find ourselves surprised at our reactions to a Gospel scene. One man, for example, was reading the section in Mark 3 that says:

> He went up the mountain and called to him those whom he wanted, and they came to him. And he appointed twelve, whom he also named apostles, to be with him, and to be sent out to proclaim the message, and to have authority to cast out demons. (Mark 3:13–15)

He found himself getting angry, and he did not understand why. He asked the Lord to help him to understand what was happening. Gradually, it dawned on him that a Christian does not have much choice about who his companions are going to be. He realized that he was angry with a number of the people with whom his Christian living had brought him together. The resentment had been building up unawares and affecting his happiness and his effectiveness in work. The realization in itself freed him of some of his malaise, and he was able to ask Jesus to help him to look at his companions as also Jesus' companions.

Another example: People are often surprised at how difficult it is to let Jesus wash their feet, as he washed the feet of his disciples at the Last Supper (John 13:1–11). When they recoil, they now understand Peter's reaction that before had seemed incomprehensible. As they ponder their reaction and ask the Lord to shine a light on it, they come to sense that their real sin is their unwillingness to accept Jesus' forgiveness and to believe that they are loved and, therefore, lovable.

People obviously differ in their imaginative abilities, or perhaps better, in the kind of imagination they have. Some seem able to visualize a whole Gospel scene in colorful detail, almost as though their imaginations are creating a Technicolor movie. Others have such vivid auditory imaginations that entire conversations go on in their heads and hearts. Others, and here I count myself, do not seem to see or hear much at all, but feel the story and the characters in a way that is hard to describe. This last group can be envious when they listen to the more vivid descriptions of others and may even feel discouraged at their "lack of imagination." Actually, everyone has an imagination. If we wince when someone describes the impact of a hammer on his thumb, we have an imagination; if we can enjoy a good story, we have an imagination. Imaginations differ, and we need to let God use the one we have and not bemoan the one we do not have.

Some people with vivid, creative imaginations have been able to let God use this gift as a way to develop the relationship. One woman I know spent a good part of a retreat on a vacation with Jesus, during which time she was able to pour out her heart to him and ask his advice about how to handle some of the troubling issues of her life. Some of her times of imaginative prayer were spent outdoors, and some were spent in front of a fireplace. Near the end of the retreat, Jesus left and headed back to the city, and she knew that this was his way of telling her that he would be with her in her daily life.

One man spent a long time in prayer on a camping trip with Jesus. During the course of the trip, the basic issue of their relationship emerged; namely, the degree of the man's ability and willingness to trust Jesus enough to tell him what was really on his mind. Some people create whole stories out of incidents in the Gospels. One woman followed Jesus on the way of the cross in vivid detail, even to the point of helping him to his feet when he stumbled and staying close to him when the guards became menacing and tried to drive her away. Nothing could keep her from going with Jesus.

When we use our imaginations in prayer, we are aware that much of what happens is based on our own past experience. How can we be sure that the whole thing is not just a fanciful daydream that we piously call prayer? I would first suggest that we trust in tradition. God has, it seems, used the imaginations of saints such as Ignatius of Loyola, Francis Xavier, and Margaret Mary Alacoque to draw them into a deep intimate friendship with God. Then I would point to a need for discernment, a discernment that does not start with being suspicious of our human nature, but rather with trusting that God has made us good.

It is a profound insight on the part of Ignatius to note in the beginning of his rules for discernment that God's presence to those who are searching for him is signaled by positive emotions: gentleness, peacefulness, quiet confidence [nn. 315–316]. If our use of imagination leads to such feelings as well as to increased faith, hope, love, and a desire to know God

and Jesus more, then we can be confident that the
Lord is using our imaginations for his purposes and
our good. Doubts about such prayer can be seen as
temptations, especially if the doubts and questions
allow for no clear answers; that is, if they remain
nagging doubts and questions and do not lead to
new and better ways to pray.

In this matter of discernment, it also helps to have
someone we can talk to about our prayer, specifically
a spiritual director.[5] For now, it suffices to note that
people's confidence in the direction of their prayer
life is helped by being able to describe their prayer
experience to someone who is interested in listening
to it. Just the act of describing to another what happens
when they pray helps them to be more attentive to
their conscious relationship with God and more
appreciative of the gifts they have been given, even if
the other person does nothing more than listen
attentively and sympathetically. In the process of
describing their experience, they often see where God
is leading them and where they are straying from the
path. It is even more helpful, of course, if the spiritual
director can also help them, by judicious questions
and comments, to see that their prayer is leading
toward a deeper intimacy with the Lord, an intimacy
that fits the pattern of how God has dealt with people

generally as well as in the unique events of their personal past.

The main point of this chapter is to encourage directors to be as free as Ignatius in supporting people in their use of whatever helps them to meet the living God. In the Ignatian tradition, imagination has been a great help. If this is their way, we must let them trust it as one of God's gifts to help them to know God better.

CHAPTER 7

The Second Week and the Historical Jesus

Ignatius was a man of his time, and he contemplated the Gospels as a man of his time. The scriptural exegesis he knew would never have questioned that the events depicted in the Gospels happened. No one in his time would have wondered how much we can know about the historical Jesus; they would have presumed the historical accuracy of the Gospel texts. We, and those we direct, live in a different world. Most educated Christians of our era have been exposed to some of the questions raised by modern scriptural scholarship. In addition, most educated Christians have been infected with the "hermeneutic of suspicion," a way of interpreting everything with suspicion, not only as to its historical accuracy, but also as to its psychological meaning.

For example, most educated people have been exposed to the kind of psychological interpretation that questions the "real" motivation behind all human action. In addition, cover stories about the historical Jesus in such weekly newsmagazines as *Time* have exposed many Christians to the "findings" of such groups as the "Jesus Seminar," which raise significant questions about how much, if anything, we can know about the historical Jesus. I believe that as directors, we need to be aware of the effects of this pervasive atmosphere of critical suspicion on those who make the Spiritual Exercises in our day.

Let me give one example. An experienced spiritual director who had done graduate studies in theology began her retreat a few years ago much distressed because of a conversation she had had with another woman who was studying theology in a divinity school. The latter had participated in a seminar about the Resurrection in which the prevailing opinion among faculty and students was that the Resurrection meant that Jesus lived on in our memories, not so much that anything had happened to Jesus himself. The woman who was beginning her retreat was deeply disturbed. If this were true, then she had based her life and her hopes on nothing more substantial than the continuing remembrance of Jesus by the Christians.

Moreover, if this were true of Jesus, it was also true of her loved ones who had died. Remembrance by their loved ones was the only "resurrected life" there was. I do not believe that this is an isolated case. Many, if not most, of our directees are infected by the hermeneutic of suspicion and the postmodern questioning of the truth of any belief.

What are we to do? In this short chapter, I cannot examine the whole question of how we know the truth of anything, especially of anything historical. Suffice it to say that it is possible to develop an interpretive method that takes modern epistemological, historical, and psychological theories of knowledge into account and yet allows us to affirm historical, philosophical, and theological truth with relative assurance.[1] Notice that I used the words *relative assurance.* We cannot have absolute certitude about historical realities; we can, however, come to a relatively sure judgment about them. We do not have to drown in the sea of relativity and suspicion that so pervades modern culture. In the case of the woman just mentioned, I took her crisis seriously and mentioned that Christian faith expressly believes that something happened to Jesus in the Resurrection. We have no proof of that except our faith and the experience based on our faith. I then urged her to speak with Jesus about her fears and anxieties. I write this short paragraph to reassure directors that post-modern skepticism is not the final word.

In addition to being immersed in this atmosphere of skepticism with regard to certain knowledge of anything, modern educated Christians are aware of the layers of redaction that have produced our four Gospels and thus may wonder how to interpret the meaning of any particular passage. Directors would be well advised to have a somewhat sophisticated grasp of the various ways a passage of the Gospels can be interpreted. For example, it could be interpreted as an actual happening in the life of Jesus of Nazareth, or as part of the argument of this particular Gospel, or as a message for the community addressed by this particular Gospel.

At the same time, the complexity of possible interpretations of a text need not incapacitate praying people in the use of Gospel passages for prayer, especially in the Second Week of the Spiritual Exercises, when the person desires to know Jesus more intimately in order to love him more intensely and follow him more closely. The Gospel stories, in other words, can be used, even in this age of more sophisticated knowledge of their redaction history, to elicit a response of faith in and love for Jesus. We can confidently use the Ignatian method of imaginative contemplation of the Gospels as a privileged way to know Jesus more intimately.[2]

One of the questions that has intrigued me in recent years is precisely what we can know through the Gospels about the historical Jesus of Nazareth. I have come to the conclusion that people can be helped in their desire to know Jesus more intimately by a director's judicious use of what I consider the best of the modern search for the historical Jesus. In *Who Do You Say I Am?*[3] I used the work of John Meier[4] as a background for helping readers to use the Gospels in order to get to know Jesus of Nazareth more intimately. More recently, in three chapters of *With an Everlasting Love,*[5] I made use of the work of N. T. Wright[6] for the same purpose. In this chapter, I want to give a short précis of how directors might use some of this material in directing the Second Week of the Spiritual Exercises.

First, let it be said that many of us find it difficult to take Jesus seriously as a human being in spite of what we avow in our theology. In childhood, we heard Jesus' name spoken with awe and reverence. We were taught to genuflect before his divine presence in the tabernacle, to bow our heads at the mention of his name. Of course, we were taught that he was a human being, but the greatest emphasis was on his divinity. We would not easily think of his needing to be toilet trained, for example, or of his learning to speak his native language. Stress was laid on his divine knowledge to such an extent that it was difficult for us to imagine his having to discover his vocation. As we help people with the desire of the Second Week, therefore, we must be aware of the difficulties we and they face in taking seriously the fact that Jesus was a human being like us in all things except sin.

One might say, at this point, that not taking this fact seriously is a small matter. I wonder. If Jesus is not human in the ways that we are human, then it lies close to hand to consider him something of a superman. In fact, a seminarian who heard me give some talks on the humanity of Jesus of Nazareth said, "If he's not human as I am, then I do not have to take him seriously as a model to emulate." I believe that this seminarian touched a raw nerve. If Jesus is superhuman, then I can admire him, but I do not have to take seriously his call to emulate him. I can never be a superhuman being.

When I direct people in the Second Week of the Exercises these days, I remind them that Jesus was just as human as they are. It is only human not to know the future, for example, or to have to discover one's vocation in life through prayer, reflection, and experience. It is only human to be so immersed in a culture that one soaks up the glories and the prejudices of that culture. It is only human to put one's trust in other human beings and to discover that they are not trustworthy. I do not give instruction at any length, but I do point out things such as these.

For example, I might mention that Jesus had to come to grips with his awakening sexuality during adolescence and that we can speak to him about our own growth into mature sexual beings. In talking about Jesus and John the Baptist, I mention that it appears that John was Jesus' mentor and indicate that this relationship could be a fruitful topic of conversation with Jesus. When I suggest the temptation in the desert, I might say that these temptations came right after Jesus' vocation as Messiah was confirmed at his baptism in the Jordan; the temptations can be looked upon as temptations to be the Messiah that many people expected. I might point out that Jesus' family wondered about his sanity, at least according to Mark's Gospel, and leave the retreatant to ask Jesus how it felt for him to be suspected of madness because of his belief in his own vocation.

When we come to passages that indicate Jesus' awareness of his unique relationship with God, and even an identity with God, I might say something like: "I wonder how he came to such a human consciousness of himself. He might even have wondered about his own sanity." As the storm clouds around Jesus grow darker, I might underline that Jesus moved forward in faith that his way of being Messiah is God's way; he had no guarantee except his trust in God and in his own relationship with God. The agony in the Garden, for example, might well have been his last struggle with the question of whether he had rightly discerned his vocation from God. After all, there was no category of crucified Messiah, which would have been, by definition, a false Messiah.

These are some suggestions for how one might approach the contemplations of the Second and Third Weeks. I have found that people grow in their appreciation and love of Jesus as they contemplate him in this way. Moreover, they see more clearly what it means to follow him more closely. I can only encourage directors to take the humanity of Jesus seriously. A Christology from below—that is, one that starts with the humanity of Jesus—can, in fact, lead to a very high Christology—that is, one that gapes in awe at the divine image presented by Jesus of Nazareth. N. T. Wright makes this point quite trenchantly.

Western orthodoxy has for too long had an overly lofty, detached and oppressive view of God. It has always tended to approach christology by assuming this view of God, and trying to fit Jesus into it. The result has been a docetic Jesus—that is, a Jesus who only seems to be truly human, but in fact is not. My proposal is not that we know what the word "God" means, and manage somehow to fit Jesus into that. Instead, I suggest that we think historically about a young Jew, possessed of a desperately risky, indeed apparently crazy, vocation, riding into Jerusalem, denouncing the Temple, dining once more with his friends, and dying on a Roman cross—and that we somehow allow our meaning of the word "God" to be re-centered on that point.[7]

We and those we direct have a chance to come closer to the true meaning of the word *God* by asking Jesus to reveal himself as a fully human Jew of the first century of our era. If we do, we will be drawn into the Mystery we call God and be surprised by what we discover.

CHAPTER 8

The Discernment of Spirits

Ignatius of Loyola lived in an age comparable to our own in its turmoil and promise. He, too, lived on the cusp as one world order crumbled and a new one was struggling to be born. One could say that he was one of the religious geniuses the Catholic Church needed at that time to see its way into the new world being born during his lifetime. His genius lay in realizing that God can be found in all things, that every human experience has a religious dimension, a religious meaning, for those who want to discover it. This discovery of the religious meaning of one's inner experience is called the discernment of spirits, a term that was rich in tradition long before the life of Ignatius, but one that received new impetus and use with the publication of the

Spiritual Exercises. In this book, Ignatius codified "Rules for the Discernment of Spirits," which he learned from his own experience [nn. 313–336]. But because discernment of spirits is often viewed as an arcane and mysterious process, something left to the mystics and masters of spirituality, we need to look more closely at this process to see how it can become an ordinary event in the life of any Christian.

Ignatius's Own Discernment

In the last chapter, we referred to Ignatius's first discernment of spirits. He noticed that two sets of daydreams led to different affective states, and he drew the conclusion that God was leading him toward a new way of life, away from the life of chivalry that gave him so much apparent pleasure. The interesting point about this first discernment is that it occurred to a layman quite innocent of any theological or spiritual knowledge. Moreover, it happened in the ordinary event of daydreaming. Nothing could be further from the esoteric or the mystical as these are ordinarily understood. Thus, we have in this story a description of the discernment of spirits in ordinary life, a description that lays to rest any theory of the discernment of spirits that makes it an esoteric or arcane spiritual discipline open only to the spiritually gifted and theologically trained. Ignatius was theologically ignorant and was so far from being spiritually gifted that even after this first discernment and a vision of the Madonna, he could not make up his mind about whether or not to kill a Moor, as a story from a chapter of his autobiography attests.

Right after he left Loyola to take up his new life of following Jesus, he and a Moor met on the road, both riding mules. They began to converse, and the conversation turned to the topic of Mary, the mother of Jesus. The Moor could well imagine that Mary had conceived Jesus without the benefit of a man, but he could not agree that she was a virgin after giving birth. Ignatius tried to dissuade him from this opinion, but could not succeed. The *Autobiography* tells us that the Moor raced on ahead of Ignatius. We can imagine that the Moor felt Ignatius getting more and more irate.

After the Moor left, Ignatius began to have misgivings about his behavior; perhaps he had not done enough to uphold the honor of our Lady. The desire came over him to race after the Moor and strike him with his dagger, but he couldn't make up his mind. He couldn't discern what to do, in other words, and he was in an agony of indecision. Finally, in desperation he decided to let the mule make the decision for him.

He let the reins go slack. If the mule followed the broad road to the town to which the Moor was heading, Ignatius would seek him out and strike him; if the mule kept to the road he was on, then he would let the Moor go. The mule kept to the road he was on.[1] Obviously, Ignatius did not immediately become a master of discernment.

Nonetheless, with the discernment he made on his sickbed we have the essential elements for an understanding of Ignatian discernment. Life is a battleground where the stakes are enormous. The two great protagonists in this battle are God and Satan. Both are in a dialogical relationship with all human beings, but for absolutely different ends. God wants all human beings to live as God's sons and daughters, as brothers and sisters of Jesus Christ. In other words, God wants all human beings to be saved, and God is working all the time in this world to achieve that end. Satan diametrically opposes God's purpose. He wants to estrange all human beings not only from God but also from one another. The battlegrounds are the hearts and minds of human beings.

Thus, for Ignatius, the struggle is dialogical; God is trying to draw human beings into the inner life of the Trinity, and Satan is trying to draw us away from that community. In ordinary human experience, both

God and the Evil One are at their work of attracting us. Hence, the influences of the two great protagonists can be discerned in ordinary human experience. Nothing in human experience is, for Ignatius, insignificant, because at every moment God and Satan are at work. Careful attention to inner experience, therefore, is a hallmark of Ignatian spirituality; such attention is absolutely necessary if the individual wants to know God's desires for him or her.

Of course, Ignatius was only taking the Gospels seriously. In *A Marginal Jew,* John Meier writes of Jesus of Nazareth:

> it is important to realize that, in the view of Jesus, . . . human beings were not basically neutral territories that might be influenced by divine or demonic forces now and then. . . . Human existence was seen as a battlefield dominated by one or the other supernatural force, God or Satan (alias Belial or the devil). A human being might have a part in choosing which "field of force" would dominate his or her life, i.e., which force he or she would choose to side with. But no human being was free to choose simply to be free of these supernatural forces. One was dominated by either one or the other, and to pass *from* one was necessarily to pass *into* the control of the other. At least over the long term, one could not maintain a neutral stance vis-à-vis God and Satan.[2]

This aspect of Ignatius's spirituality has great relevance for our own age. We are in an age in which many of the institutions, structures, and customs by which people lived their lives without much thought have been called into question. There are few outside criteria by which men and women of today can make clear decisions about right and wrong, about the better way to live their lives, etc. Moreover, as John Macmurray long ago pointed out, our civilization has arrived at the point where our intellects are refined and highly honed but our emotions (our hearts) are relatively undeveloped and immature. In a trenchant series of BBC broadcasts in the early 1930s, he argued forcefully that Westerners needed to submit to the discipline of developing more adult and civilized hearts.[3] The genius of this sixteenth-century saint, Ignatius of Loyola, still has relevance for our day.

Another aspect of this spirituality may be much more difficult for modern men and women to accept. At Manresa, Ignatius was tutored by God and gradually became a master of discernment. During these months of prayer, he became convinced that God wanted him to live out his days in Jerusalem, and with the single-mindedness so characteristic of him, he proceeded to go there. "He made a firm decision to remain in Jerusalem, constantly visiting the Holy

Places. In addition to this devout desire of his, he was also intent on helping souls."[4] When the provincial of the Franciscans told him that he could not remain, Ignatius told him quite frankly that he was determined to stay. Only when the provincial threatened him with excommunication did Ignatius agree to obey, concluding that "it was not Our Lord's will for him to remain in the Holy Places."[5]

Leo Bakker, commenting on the Rules for Discernment, maintains that Ignatius's decision to remain in Jerusalem was made around the time of his vision by the River Cardoner and was an election in the First Time; that is, "an occasion when God our Lord moves and attracts the will in such a way that a devout person, without doubting or being able to doubt, carries out what was proposed" [n. 175]. According to Bakker, the Jerusalem provincial's decision led Ignatius to question how a decision that was clearly God's (his election to stay in Jerusalem) could be contrary to a decision that was clearly God's (the provincial's decision). In Bakker's view, reflection on this question led to the Eighth Rule of the rules for discernment, more suitable to the Second Week of the Exercises [n. 336], in which Ignatius cautions the exercitant to distinguish carefully the moment of a consolation from succeeding moments.[6] Bakker also traces the Rules for Thinking with the Church in the Spiritual Exercises [nn. 352–370] to this experience in Jerusalem.

For Ignatius, authority in the church was clearly a mediator of the will of God. Discernment of spirits was always in creative tension with obedience to legitimate authority as a means of knowing God's will. For many modern Christians, Catholics among them, authority does not have the same sharp relevance that it had for Ignatius. Many would find inexplicable the complete acquiescence of a man of such obvious strength of character to the provincial's authority. Yet Ignatian discernment must be understood as embedded in the "Catholic thing," in the belief that the institutional church also mediates the will of God. Ignatian spirituality is decidedly realistic and Catholic. Discernment takes place in the real world, where all things are not possible, and in the Catholic Church, where legitimate authority may have the final word.

Discernment and the Principle and Foundation

Now let us develop at more length some of the central elements of Ignatian discernment of spirits. First, the discernment of spirits must be understood against the background of the First Principle and

Foundation, the "Fundamentum" elucidated by Joseph Tetlow.[7] Tetlow argues, as we noted in chapter 4, that behind the seemingly dry and catechism-like words of Ignatius lies an experience of God's creative and continually creating action. God is always actively working to bring about God's kingdom, and we can be in tune, out of tune, or more or less in tune with God's intention. With absolute clarity and consequentiality, Ignatius saw that, for our own best interests and blessedness, we need to be in tune with God's one action.

The First Principle and Foundation is a pithy statement of this insight. Let me paraphrase the first two sentences of the Principle in the language of this chapter. "Human beings are created for community with the Trinity and hence with one another. All the other things on the face of the earth are created to help us to attain this community." We have to understand this statement not as an external demand put on human beings by a sovereign and implacable God, but as an expression of what is for our good. The Spiritual Exercises are a means to becoming attuned to God's one action and intention, to becoming contemplatives in action, people who quite literally find God in all things, even in the hurly-burly of an active life.

Discernment and Action

Historically, the purpose of the Exercises has been understood in two different senses. One tendency stressed the aim of union with God; the other stressed the discovery of God's will. In agreement with Bakker and other modern commentators, I prefer to join the two and see the Spiritual Exercises as a means of helping people to achieve union with God in action. Bakker notes, for example, that for Ignatius, consolation was not first and foremost a pleasant and moving emotion, nor encouragement to continue on a chosen path, nor help in prayer; consolation includes all of these, but first and foremost it is an experience that makes it possible to know and choose the will of God.

> From the time of the illumination at Cardoner the discernment of inner movements and consolation flow together with the election (e.g., the choice of a way of life) for Ignatius. The fact that Ignatius reflexively emphasizes this flowing together of consolation and election and then methodically works it out as the center and source of the spiritual life is the new element brought into the history of spirituality by the Spiritual Exercises.[8]

In other words, in Ignatian spirituality, union with God occurs in the decision to act in a certain way and in the action itself. In Macmurray's terminology, we become one with God insofar as we are in tune with the one action of God in our own actions. To put it another way, we become one with God insofar as our actions are in tune with the kingdom of God.[9]

In the *Autobiography,* Ignatius tells us that he learned to distrust consolations that came to him as he was about to go to sleep. These consolations kept him from the little sleep he had allotted to himself.

> Now and then reflecting on this loss of sleep, he considered how he had allotted a fixed amount of time each day to converse with God, and then the remainder of the day as well, and thus he came to doubt whether those lights came from the good spirit. He concluded that it was better to set them aside and sleep the allotted time. This he did.[10]

Later, in Barcelona and in Paris, he found that consolations kept him from paying attention in class or from memorizing his grammar lessons. Gradually, he came to the conclusion that these "consolations" also were temptations.[11] In these two vignettes, we see how deeply Ignatius had penetrated the mystery of God's action in this world. Even profound spiritual "consolations" can be discovered to be temptations by reference to their deleterious effects on action that one has discerned to be in tune with God's one action. Asceticism requires that one eschew such "consolations" in order to be in union with God.

For Ignatius, the discernment of spirits became so important in ordinary life that he frequently made examinations of consciousness.[12] Moreover, he would allow a Jesuit to miss all other spiritual exercises for the sake of the apostolate except the examination of consciousness (the examen). For Ignatius, the examen functioned much as the period of reflection after each prayer time in the Spiritual Exercises. Just as the person making the Exercises is asked to reflect on the period of prayer in order to discern the movements of the spirits, so too, for Ignatius, the contemplative in action, could a period of the day be considered a time of encountering the different spirits. Thus he reflected on that period to discover the movements of these spirits.

Rules for Discernment

For our own good, God desires that the actions of each of us be in tune with God's one action; in our best moments, we too desire to be in tune with God's action. How do we know whether we are in tune or not? I believe that when we are out of tune with God's one action, we experience ourselves as alienated, unhappy, and unfulfilled even though we do not know the source of the malaise. These feelings of malaise are, I believe, what Ignatius calls the actions of the "good spirit" in his First Rule for the Discernment of Spirits.

> In the case of persons who are going from one mortal sin to another, the enemy ordinarily proposes to them apparent pleasures. He makes them imagine delights and pleasures of the senses, in order to hold them fast and plunge them deeper into their sins and vices.

> But with persons of this type the good spirit uses a contrary procedure. Through their good judgment on problems of morality he stings their consciences with remorse. [n. 314]

In other words, when I am out of tune with the one action of God, when I am acting predominantly out of fear for myself and, therefore, against the community of the Trinity, rather than out of love for others, then I experience the action of God as a troubling of my spirit, as a sting of conscience. Ignatius's own experience of sadness after the daydreams about knightly deeds is an example of this action of God. God continually acts in the universe to draw all of us into community with the Trinity and with one another. When we act counter to that action, we experience ourselves as somehow out of sorts with ourselves and with others. In this understanding, there is no need of special interventions by God or the good spirit, although we may experience the one action of God as an external intervention.

The Second Rule for the Discernment of Spirits in the Exercises speaks "of persons who are earnestly purging away their sins, and who are progressing from good to better in the service of God our Lord." In our terminology, these are people who desire to attune their actions with the one action of God and desire it effectively. In this case, Ignatius says:

> it is characteristic of the evil spirit to cause gnawing anxiety, to sadden, and to set up obstacles. In this way he unsettles these persons by false reasons aimed at preventing their progress.

> But with persons of this type it is characteristic of the good spirit to stir up courage and strength, consolations, tears, inspirations, and tranquility. He makes things easier and eliminates all obstacles, so that the persons may move forward in doing good. [n. 315]

Can we make sense of this for our times? In an earlier book, I answered the question in this way:

If you have ever experienced a time when you were "in the flow," able to live with relative unambivalence and lack of fear in the now, attuned to the presence of God, then you have an idea of what it might be like to be at one with the one action of God. In such a state you are a contemplative in action. You know that you are at the right place at the right time. There are no doubts about whether you should be someone else or somewhere else. You do not need to justify being married or single or a religious; it is right to be who you are here and now. And you live and act comfortably with the knowledge of your own limitations, of your finitude, of your small part in the immense history of the world. To be attuned to the one action of God, to his will, is to be extraordinarily free, happy and fulfilled even in the midst of a world of sorrow and pain. One can, perhaps, understand how Jesus could celebrate the Last Supper even though he knew in his bones that it would be "last."[13]

To be in tune with God's intention in this way is to experience what Ignatius calls "consolation" in the next rule.

By [this kind of] consolation I mean that which occurs when some interior motion is caused within the soul through which it comes to be inflamed with love of its Creator and Lord. As a result it can love no created thing on the face of the earth in itself, but only in the Creator of them all.

Similarly, this consolation is experienced when the soul sheds tears which move it to love for its Lord—whether they are tears of grief for its own sins, or about the Passion of Christ our Lord, or about other matters directly ordered to his service and praise.

Finally, under the word consolation I include every increase in hope, faith, and charity, and every interior joy which calls and attracts one toward heavenly things and to the salvation of one's soul, by bringing it tranquility and peace in its Creator and Lord. [n. 316]

With Josef Sudbrack, we can equate the modern concept of identity with Ignatius's concept of consolation.[14] According to this theory, the best criterion for discerning whether or not we are in tune with God's one action in our daily choices is the sense of developing inner and outer harmony, a growing sense of ourselves as related harmoniously to other people, our world, and our God. A person who has made it a habit to discern in this manner is well on the way to being a contemplative in action.

To be out of tune with God's intention is to experience what Ignatius calls "desolation" in the Fourth Rule.

By [this kind of] desolation I mean everything which is the contrary of what was described in the Third Rule; for example, obtuseness of soul, turmoil within it, an

> impulsive motion toward low and earthly things, or dis-
> quiet from various agitations and temptations. These
> move one toward lack of faith and leave one without
> hope and without love. One is completely listless,
> tepid, and unhappy, and feels separated from our
> Creator and Lord. [n. 317]

I believe that it is easy enough to recognize such desolation when its source is personal sinfulness, when
the person is personally alienated from God's intention. What directors need to be alert to is the possibility that such desolation comes from a sense of
hopelessness about the person's social life.

Alienation from institutions is pervasive in our
society. We see corruption all around us, in govern-
ment, in business, and even in the churches. There is
a wholesale lack of trust not only of "City Hall"
(meaning any institution that governs), but also of fellow citizens. Crime in the streets, in schools, and in
our homes is an everyday affair. Anger and hatred
often seem only barely concealed, and violence only
avoided with great control. Many, if not most, of us
experience a sense of frustration and helplessness
about the structures and patterns that govern our
lives. We may also vaguely feel a complicity in these
structures or patterns. For example, race and class
seem to keep so many of our fellow citizens trapped

in the inner cities of our country. We become aware of the possibility that we ourselves are part of the problem, not of the solution. Such feelings can make prayer difficult, if not impossible.

However, if these feelings do not lead to a deeper conversation with the Lord and to a concerted effort to do our part to change the sinful social structures that condition our lives as a people, then they are desolation—what I would call, for lack of a better term, "social desolation." When we encounter such desolation in ourselves or in those we direct, we need to bring these feelings of helplessness and hopelessness to the Lord for healing. At a meeting in Brussels on the Spiritual Exercises, Gerard W. Hughes, S.J., made an interesting observation. He has found that people who have spent time working for social justice often feel "shame and confusion" during the First Week (what they desire in the First Week, [n. 48]) because of the sorry state of the society they are part of. Interestingly enough, this shame and confusion is liberating; they discover that God does not want the society to be so unjust, but that God still loves the world and this society and wants people who will work to change it.

An Example That Illustrates the Use of the Rules

It would take us too far afield to go through all the Rules for Discernment in the Spiritual Exercises. What I want to show here is that these rules are not esoteric or out of the ordinary. They can be verified in our ordinary lives if we take the time to pay attention to our experience. A recent novel, *Glamorous Powers* by Susan Howatch, might well be read as a description of the discernment of spirits. It reads like a spiritual mystery story.

Two of Ignatius's rules can be illustrated by one section of the novel. The protagonist is Father Darrow, an abbot of the Fordite Congregation noted for his psychic and spiritual gifts (the "glamorous powers" of the title). On the occasion of the death of Darrow's mentor, the founder of the Fordites, and the accession of his rival, Father Francis, to the office of Abbot-General, Darrow has a vision that he interprets as a call to leave the Fordites and return to life as a priest in the "world." Abbot Francis, however, has doubts about the authenticity of the call and demands that Darrow enter into a period of discernment with him. Darrow tries to use his psychic powers and his self-control to bend the process of discernment toward his interpretation of the vision. He even lies to Abbot Francis. In the Thirteenth

Rule of the Rules for the First Week [n. 326], Ignatius notes that the bad spirit tries to seduce a person into secrecy about what is actually happening in his or her experience. In the First Rule of the Rules for the Second Week, he notes that "it is characteristic of the enemy to fight against this happiness and spiritual consolation, by using specious reasonings, subtleties, and persistent deceits" [n. 329]. In his attempts to sidetrack an authentic discernment of spirits, Darrow becomes an angry and very unhappy man. The turn toward real discernment comes in the following scene. Darrow is narrating.

> "I lied to you yesterday," I said to Francis when we met again. "I'm sorry. I know very well I've got to be entirely truthful in order to help you reach the right decision."
>
> Francis never asked what the lie was. That impressed me. Nor did he make any attempt to humiliate me further by embarking on a justifiable reproof. That impressed me even more. Instead he motioned me to sit down and said abruptly: "It's a question of trust, isn't it, and you don't trust me yet."
>
> I forced myself to say: "I do want to trust you."
>
> "Well, at least that's a step in the right direction."
>
> "And I do accept that you're a first-class monk—"

"No, you don't. You accept that I'm a first-class administrator and you accept that the old man gave me a first-class training, but I've still to prove I'm a first-class monk, and that's why it's just as vital for me as it is for you that I should deal with your crisis correctly. I know perfectly well that you believe the only reason why I became Abbot-General was because I knew how to exploit the old man's secret longing for a son. Well, now I have to prove the old man wasn't completely off his head and that I really am the right man for the job, so accept that I have a powerful motive to behave properly here, Jonathan, and do please discard your fear that I'll be unable to wield the charism of discernment unless you regularly throw in a lie or two to help me along."

Yet again I was impressed. I heard myself say: "It takes courage to be as honest as that. Thank you. I can't promise you I'll succeed in matching your honesty, but I can promise I'll do my best to try."

"Then put on your boxing-gloves," said Francis, not ill-pleased by this exchange, "and let's step back into the ring for the next round."[15]

The novel as a whole concerns Darrow's struggle to discern the meaning of his vocation.

Conclusion

On his sickbed, Ignatius had two sets of daydreams that had different repercussions in his emotional life. One day, he noticed the difference and then decided that one set of daydreams was from God and the other wasn't. Yet God was also in the worldly daydreams, as the Spirit that left him feeling disconsolate afterward. From these simple beginnings, Ignatian spirituality developed. Ignatius learned from experience that God could be found in all things. The phrase "finding God in all things" has become a hallmark of Ignatian spirituality. What Ignatius learned on his sickbed and later is part of the heritage of the church's tradition. It still has relevance for our own time. We must only begin to pay attention to our experience and ask where God is present in it.

CHAPTER 9

The Changing Self-God Image of Ignatius in Relation to Discernment

Since the assimilation of modern psychology into contemporary spirituality, many have attempted to describe the developing relationship between a person and God in interpersonal terms.[1] Those of us who use such a framework often use a form of what Freudians call "object relations theory" and apply it to the relationship with God.[2] According to this theory, we all carry around with us self-other schemata (internal "images" or psychic structures of the self in relation to others) learned in our interactions with significant people. We approach all new people within the context of these schemata. Such a theory serves to explain instant likes and dislikes. A new person is assimilated into an image of someone in my past life whom I liked or disliked. The theory is also used to explain how people get into repetitive destructive relationships without ever learning from experience. These schemata are self-other psychic structures; they are relational in nature because they are learned through relationships. In other words, these psychological structures with their associated feelings and thoughts are of the self in relation to another and others. All our self-images are relational.

According to this theory, we also meet God with learned self-God schemata that derive from our relationships with parents and others, from teachings about God, and from past experiences of the Mystery we call God.[3] These schemata are always distorted and untrue to the reality of who God really is for us. In other words, our experience of God is impoverished because of our self-God schemata. We could say that the development of the relationship with God consists in progressively learning more realistic images of self and God in relationship through the actual encounter with God in sacraments, prayer, and other life experiences. The development could be seen as a process of losing our idols or false images of God (and self) through the encounter itself just as the encounter with a new person in our life will teach us something new about ourselves and that person if we let the relationship develop.

I contend that one criterion for assessing whether people are heading in the right direction in their lives might be the quality of their relationship with God and the changes that have taken place in their relationship with God. Thus shifts in a person's self-God schema could be used to discern whether or not experiences are of God and whether the thrust of a person's life is moving forward or regressing.

In this chapter, I want to illustrate such a progression by using the *Autobiography* of Ignatius. I believe that the experiences Ignatius describes in the first three chapters of that work can be understood in terms of Ignatius's progressive education about his relationship with God. In other words, the changes he describes can be understood as changes in his self-God schema. In the course of demonstrating this thesis, we will discover that Ignatius, who calls himself the pilgrim in the *Autobiography,* shows himself to be a pilgrim from an impoverished image of God to an image of God as lover par excellence. In the process, his own self-image changes as well.

First, let us once again note that Ignatius's initial conversion experience came about through noticing the

difference between two sets of daydreams as he conva-
lesced from his wounds and leg operations. In one set
of daydreams, Ignatius spent hours on end imagining
the great deeds he would do and the fine words he
would say to win the heart of a great lady. In the other
set, Ignatius spent equally long hours dreaming of the
great deeds he would do for Christ in imitation of saints
such as Dominic and Francis. He noted that there was
a difference between the two experiences.

> When he thought of worldly matters he found much
> delight, but after growing weary and dismissing them
> he found that he was dry and unhappy. But when he
> thought of going barefoot to Jerusalem and of eating
> nothing but vegetables and of imitating the saints in all
> the austerities they performed, he not only found con-
> solation in these thoughts but even after they had left
> him he remained happy and joyful. He did not con-
> sider nor did he stop to examine this difference until
> one day his eyes were partially opened and he began to
> wonder at this difference and to reflect upon it. From
> experience he knew that some thoughts left him sad
> while others made him happy, and little by little he came
> to perceive the different spirits that were moving him; one
> coming from the devil, the other coming from God.[4]

In these two sets of daydreams, the same vaulting
ambition and the same vivid imagination are at work,

but to different ends. The life of Christ and the lives of the saints piqued Ignatius's interest and fired his imagination much as did the romantic literature he so enjoyed and would have preferred to read during his convalescence. Finally, he noticed that the two sets of daydreams had different emotional consequences in his heart, and then he discerned that one set was from God while the other was from the demon.

With this decisive discernment, Ignatius was set upon a new path, but he was not yet a new person. The rather amusing story recounted earlier of his encounter with the Moor on the road to Montserrat shows how far he was from being a man of discernment.[5] What was Ignatius's image of himself in relation to God at this time? A telling phrase occurs in the passage in which he recounts his desire to enter the Carthusian house in Seville.

> But when he again thought of the penances he wanted to fulfill as he went about the world, the desire for the Carthusian way of life cooled since he feared that there he would not be able to give vent to the *hatred* that he had conceived against himself.[6]

That self-hatred tells us much about his image of God at this time of preparation for the journey that would end up in Manresa. If Ignatius hated himself so violently, we can speculate that he harbored an image of himself before an implacable God. Not long after his arrival in Manresa, we hear ominous hints of where such a self-God image can lead.

> While in Manresa he begged alms every day. He ate no meat, nor did he drink wine, though both were offered to him. On Sundays he did not fast, and if someone gave him wine, he drank it. And because he had been quite meticulous in caring for his hair, which was according to the fashion of the day—and he had a good crop of hair—he decided to let it grow naturally without combing, cutting, or covering it with anything either during the day or night. For the same reason he let the nails of his feet and hands grow since he had also been overly neat with regard to them.[7]

He began to attack his body and his former attitudes with reckless abandon, to the point of doing permanent harm to his health, as he notes later. It is at this point that he mentions the serpent-like image that "gave him much consolation." "He received much delight and consolation from gazing upon this object and the more he looked upon it, the more his consolation increased, but when the object vanished he became disconsolate."[8] Ignatius does not make the connection with the earlier discernment, when he noted that the daydreams of doing knightly deeds delighted him during the dreaming but left him sad afterward. Moreover, he notes that around the time when this vision began, "a disturbing thought came to torment him, pointing out to him the burdensomeness of his life. It was like someone speaking within his soul: 'And how will you be able to put up with this for the seventy years you have ahead of you?'"[9] With this temptation began the great mood swings that led him into the terrible bout of scruples that he so poignantly describes in the following pages of the *Autobiography*.

The agony of his struggle with these scruples brought him to this point:

> Once, being very disturbed because of them, he set himself to pray and with great fervor he cried aloud to God, saying, "Help me, Lord, for I find no remedy among men, nor in any creature. No task would be too irksome for me if I thought I could get help. Lord, show me where I may get it, and even if I have to follow after a little dog to get the remedy I need, I will do it."

> Taken up with these thoughts he was many times vehemently tempted to throw himself into a deep hole in his room which was near the place where he used to pray.[10]

At this point, his self-hatred took a suicidal turn. What kind of God-image lies behind such scruples? It has to be that of a God who, in the words of psychiatrist J. S. Mackenzie, "is always snooping around after sinners."[11] Ignatius felt that he had not completely confessed his sins. At one point, a confessor ordered him not to confess any sin of the past "unless it was something abundantly clear. But since he considered everything manifestly clear, the order benefited him not at all."[12] For Ignatius at this time, God must have been a terrible judge ready to pounce on every sin.

Finally, Ignatius had a couple of days in which he felt free from scruples.

> But on the third day, which was Tuesday, the remembrance of his sins returned to him while he was at prayer, and as one thing leads to another, he thought of sin after sin from his past life and felt obliged to confess them again. After these thoughts, there came upon him a loathing for the life he was then living and he had a strong temptation to give it up. In this manner the Lord chose to awaken him as from a dream.[13]

Ignatius, we can speculate, realized that the image of God with which he had operated thus far in Manresa was a product of the demon and not an image of the true God. He continues:

> Now that he had some experience with the different spirits—through the lessons that God had given

him—he began to think about the way that that spirit
had come to him. Thus he decided, and with great clarity of mind, never to confess his past sins again and
from that day forward he was free of his scruples, and
he held it for certain that Our Lord had desired to set
him free because of his mercy.[14]

God is not implacable, but merciful, and Ignatius could
count on this God. Thus he didn't need to continually
grub around in his mind for possible unconfessed sins.
It is important to notice that this discernment led
Ignatius to an act of faith in who God is. He had no
guarantee that he was correct in this discernment, but
he acted on it in faith that God is not an ogre pursuing
the hapless sinner.

Immediately after recounting this discernment,
Ignatius describes how he rather easily discerned
God's will in two matters that before would have led
to agonizing indecision. The first we have already
mentioned: how he came to realize that great spiritual
consolations at bedtime were a temptation and not of
God.[15] How his image of God changed! In the next
paragraph, he describes how an experience of the
image of meat compelled him to abandon, without
any hesitation or doubt, his firm practice of never
eating meat. Even when his confessor asked him to
consider whether this was a temptation, Ignatius

could not doubt that the good spirit was the source of the image. He then says, "During this period God was dealing with him in the same way a schoolteacher deals with a child while instructing him."[16] He goes on to describe in five points the ways God revealed Godself, culminating in the description of the extraordinary enlightenment on the banks of the Cardoner. After this experience, he recognized the image of the serpent-like figure as a temptation.

The final demonstration that the encounter with God changed Ignatius's self-God schema comes in the next paragraphs, where Ignatius describes three instances in which he faced death. The first occurred at Manresa when a fever brought him to death's door. He was convinced that he was about to die.

> At that instant the thought came into his mind that he was numbered among the righteous, but this brought him so much distress that he tried everything to dismiss it and to dwell on his sins. He had more difficulty with that thought than with the fever, but no matter how much he toiled to overcome it, he was unable to do so. When the fever lessened and he was no longer in danger of death, he loudly cried out to certain ladies who had come to visit him that the next time they saw him at death's door they were, for the love of God, to shout aloud that he was a sinner and that he should be ever mindful of the sins he had committed against God.[17]

Let us contrast this experience with the next one he describes. He was on a ship from Spain to Italy, and when the ship encountered a storm, everyone on board was convinced that death was inevitable.

> Thus, making use of his time, he made a careful examination of conscience and prepared himself for death, but he felt no fear because of his sins nor was he afraid of being condemned, but he was especially disturbed and sorry, knowing that he had not put to good use all the gifts and graces that God our Lord had granted him.[18]

Now Ignatius knew that he was a sinner, and that knowledge saddened him, but it did not frighten him. He trusted in the mercy of God. The self-God image seemed to be that of a person who is convinced that he is a sinner loved and forgiven by an all-merciful God.

Then Ignatius describes a time in the year 1550, in Rome, when he and everyone else were convinced that he was about to die of a fever.

> Thinking of death at that time, he experienced such joy and such spiritual consolation in the thought of having to die that he burst into tears. This came to be of such frequent occurrence that many times he stopped thinking of death just so as not to have so much consolation.[19]

Now Ignatius seemed to be enamored of God, totally caught up with the desire for ultimate union with God. Thoughts of his sins did not seem to arise. The self-God image seemed to be that of beloved to lover. God had taught Ignatius the ultimate lesson of who God really is for Ignatius, and for all of us: lover par excellence. Fidelity to the relationship with God changed Ignatius's image of God as well as his image of himself.

Ignatius urges the one who directs the Spiritual Exercises to "allow the Creator to deal immediately with the creature and the creature with its Creator and Lord" [n. 15]. In that encounter with God, the person can learn a new and more realistic self-God schema. All of us have schemata that impoverish our experience of God and thus of ourselves. In his *Autobiography,* Ignatius shows himself as a pilgrim who moves from a small view of God to one of God as lover. Ignatius believed that the same change can happen to us.

CHAPTER 10

Touchstone Experiences as Divining Rods in Discernment

In *The Practice of Spiritual Direction,* William Connolly and I describe how Ignatius of Loyola finally recognized the demonic origin of his serpent image after his illumination at the River Cardoner, a point noted in the last chapter. We then note:

> Here we see one of the criteria that people use to decide whether an experience is of God: They compare it to another experience that they are sure is of God. Then, if they see that in some respect the two conflict, they decide which experience to accept. Many people have a touchstone experience of God. Any other experience that seems to run counter to that touchstone they look upon with suspicion. God can be so manifestly present to them during such a touchstone experience that they cannot doubt it any more than they can doubt their own existence.[1]

— 149 —

People may wonder what such experiences might be. I believe that the resurrection appearances of Jesus in the Gospels illustrate the positive use of touchstone experiences to recognize the risen Lord. Reflection on some of these stories may help us to discover our own touchstone experiences and help others to discover theirs.

Mary Magdalene saw a stranger whom she took to be a gardener. Her own love for Jesus showed itself poignantly when the "gardener" asked her:

> "Woman, why are you weeping? Whom are you looking for?" . . . "Sir, if you have carried him away, tell me where you have laid him, and I will take him away." Jesus said to her, "Mary!" She turned and said to him in Hebrew, "Rabbouni!" (which means Teacher). (John 20:15–16)

The familiar voice speaking her name instantly told her that the stranger was her beloved Jesus.

The two disciples walking sadly toward Emmaus also met a stranger who spoke meaningfully about the Scriptures and the suffering Messiah. Yet though their hearts were burning as they walked along with him, they did not recognize him. Still, they did not want to let him go when they reached their destination. Perhaps something was tugging at the sleeves of their memories. When they had prevailed on the stranger to stay for a meal with them, "he took bread, blessed and broke it, and gave it to them. Then their eyes were opened, and they recognized him" (Luke 24:30–31). The familiar gesture of blessing bread and breaking and giving it, a gesture that before the Crucifixion must have burned itself into their hearts as an archetypal experience of Jesus, let them see in this stranger the Lord whose death had dashed all their hopes. Only now did they pay attention to the fact that their hearts were burning during the whole time the stranger was with them.

In the twenty-first chapter of John's Gospel, we read that Peter and the other disciples went fishing and caught nothing all night. In the morning, a stranger "said to them, 'Cast the net to the right side of the boat, and you will find some.' So they cast it, and now they were not able to haul it in because there were so many fish. That disciple whom Jesus loved said to Peter, 'It is the Lord!'" (John 21:6–7). The Gospel writer seems to be alluding to the miraculous catch of fish that, in the synoptic Gospels, inaugurated the call of the disciples as apostles. Again, a touchstone experience of Jesus is brought back to memory and leads to the recognition of the Lord in a new situation.

I suspect that many, perhaps most, people have such touchstone experiences of God. In fact, social-science research indicates that the majority of people, at least in the United States and Great Britain, have rather powerful experiences of God.[2] But I also suspect that most of us who do have such experiences do not give them enough credit. We do not pay enough attention to them or fix them in memory. As a result, they are episodic events in our lives, like passing stomachaches, to which we pay little heed once they have passed. Hence they cannot serve as divining rods for the discernment of God's presence in new situations. I write this short chapter to encourage us to pay attention to the moments when we feel our hearts burning, as it were, and to help others to do the same.

Perhaps just reading this chapter will jog the reader's memory and bring back to mind an experience that was deeply felt and could serve as such a touchstone. On occasion, I have noticed that the very act of telling my spiritual director about an experience that had not seemed important sparks a memory of the experience that is even more powerful than the original. As they describe their experiences in direction, some people I direct come to realize that experiences that initially seemed minor are in fact profound revelations of God. Sometimes we need to be asked about experiences before we can recognize how important they are to us. The Religious Experience Research Unit at Oxford University in England, founded in 1969, has received thousands of accounts of religious experiences in response to its ads in newspapers and pamphlets. These researchers asked readers to send in records of religious experiences they had had along with relevant personal information. Replies poured in from all over Britain. Many of them are striking and could be the touchstone experiences we have been discussing. A few examples from Alister Hardy's book will give the flavor.

> I heard nothing, yet it was as if I were *surrounded by golden light* and as if I only had to reach out my hand to touch God himself who was so surrounding me with his compassion.[3]

> It seemed to me that, in some way, I was extending into my surroundings and was becoming one with them. At the same time I felt a sense of lightness, exhilaration and power as if I was beginning to understand the true meaning of the whole universe.[4]

> One night I suddenly had an experience as if I was buoyed up by waves of utterly sustaining power and love. The only words that came near to describing it were "underneath are the everlasting arms," though this sounds like a picture, and my experience was not a picture but a feeling, and there were the arms. This I

am sure has affected my life as it has made me know the love and sustaining power of God. It came from outside and unasked.[5]

On the first night I knelt to say my prayers, which I had now made a constant practice, I was aware of a glowing light which seemed to envelop me and which was accompanied by a sense of warmth all round me.[6]

Suddenly I felt a great joyousness sweeping over me. I use the word "sweeping" because this feeling seemed to do just that. I actually felt it as coming from my left and sweeping round and through me, completely engulfing me. I do not know how to describe it. It was not like a wind. But suddenly it was there, and I felt it move around and through me. Great joy was in it. Exaltation might be a better word.[7]

Whether these experiences would have meant as much to the writers had they not been asked to send them to the research unit I do not know. However, I venture to say that the interest of the unit in hearing about such experiences may well have jogged the memories of some of the writers, allowing them to recall the experiences and to savor them more deeply. Now they could be used as a kind of touchstone for discerning new experiences of God. However, these people might need the help of another person, such as a spiritual director, to see the possibility of such use.

As indicated earlier, for St. Ignatius of Loyola, the illumination at the River Cardoner seems to have been such a touchstone experience. In his *Autobiography,* he describes how he sat down at the river.

> As he sat there the eyes of his understanding were opened and though he saw no vision he understood and perceived many things, numerous spiritual things as well as matters touching on faith and learning, and this was with an elucidation so bright that all these things seemed new to him. . . . He received such a lucidity in understanding that during the course of his entire life—now having passed his sixty-second year—if he were to gather all the helps he received from God and everything he knew, and add them together, he does not think they would add up to all that he received on that one occasion.[8]

Not only does this illumination make a strong impression on Ignatius for the rest of his life, but immediately after the experience he is able to discern that the serpent-like vision that had formerly given him such comfort was a temptation. The touchstone experience at the River Cardoner enabled him to discern wheat from chaff in other experiences.

Just as Mary and the other disciples recognized the stranger as their risen Lord through some gesture that reminded them of a profound experience of Jesus, so too can all of us use the memory of touchstone experiences of God to discern whether our present experiences are of the same "stuff," as it were. But we need to savor and nourish the memories of such experiences and tell them to our spiritual directors.

Telling one's spiritual director about such experiences can have two consequences. First, as noted earlier, the telling itself can both etch the experience in memory and help us to remember even more of the experience than we initially recalled. In the telling, we remember details we had not paid attention to but that still made an impression on us. The disciples on the road to Emmaus realized that their hearts had been burning within them throughout the journey with the stranger only after the breaking of the bread. So too do we often realize the full impact of touchstone experiences only after the fact and in the telling.

Second, telling one's spiritual director can have unanticipated and beneficial consequences in future spiritual direction sessions. Often enough, I remember a directee's profound experiences when the person, because of desolation and/or resistance, does not remember them. In many such instances, I remind the person of the past experience of intense consolation either to help the person to resist the pull of profound desolation or to help him or her to discern what is happening at the present moment and to decide which experience to trust. It sometimes happens that the desolation is a resistance reaction to experiences of profound intimacy with the Lord.[9] Remembering and telling someone about profound experiences of closeness to the Lord can be a royal road to an ever-deepening intimacy.

CHAPTER 11

Toward Communal Discernment: Some Practical Suggestions

Something interesting happened in the Society of Jesus between the Thirty-first General Congregation (1965–66) and the Thirty-second (1974–75). Every reference to spiritual discernment or to the discernment of spirits in the documents of GC 31 refers to individual discernment, whereas the preponderance of such references in GC 32 are to discernment in common. GC 31 was obviously concerned with the Society recovering the dynamic of the Spiritual Exercises and especially the individual discernment of spirits. While not neglecting the need for such a continuing recovery, GC 32 made an effort to encourage communities to become communities of discernment.

> Clearly, the requisite dispositions for true communitarian discernment are such that they will not be verified as often as those for ordinary community dialogue. Nevertheless, every community should seek to acquire them, so that when need arises it can enter into this special way of seeking the will of God.[1]

What happened between 1966 and 1975?

In North America, the directed retreat movement (giving the Spiritual Exercises individually) spread like a brushfire through the Society. At GC 31, it was almost timidly suggested that "the scholastics [Jesuits studying for the priesthood] should be permitted on occasion during their formation to make the Spiritual Exercises alone under the direction of an experienced spiritual father."[2] By the time of GC 32, hardly a scholastic in North America made the Exercises in any other way. Spiritual direction with an emphasis on the discussion of the actual religious experience of the person also took on great importance.

Along with this increased interest in individual spiritual direction and this recovery of the original intention of St. Ignatius in giving the Exercises came a renewed interest in other aspects of Ignatian spirituality. The Institute of Jesuit Sources under George Ganss began publishing English translations of original Jesuit documents, the most important being the appearance in 1970 of Ganss's own translation of the *Constitutions*.[3] The Institute also made available in translation such scholarly works as de Guibert's *The Jesuits: Their Spiritual Doctrine and Practice*[4] and began publishing original studies that made it possible for English-speaking Jesuits to recover their spiritual heritage. Finally, in 1969, the American Assistancy Seminar on Jesuit Spirituality under the direction of George Ganss began publishing the influential monograph series, *Studies in the Spirituality of Jesuits.* Thus, the Society of Jesus in North America responded to the call of Vatican II that religious try to recover the charism of their founders.

Early in the *Studies* series, in April 1970, "Ignatian Discernment" by John Futrell appeared.[5] This monograph, based on Futrell's doctoral dissertation, focused not only on individual discernment but also on communal discernment modeled on the deliberation that led to the founding of the Society of Jesus. A year and a half later, Jules Toner's "A Method of Communal Discernment of God's Will"[6] was published, to be followed in November 1972 by Futrell's "Communal Discernment: Reflections on

Experience."[7] Finally, in June 1974, Toner's "The Deliberation That Started the Jesuits"[8] came out. Since that time, nothing more on communal discernment has appeared in the Studies series.

Even a cursory reading of these four publications makes it clear that Futrell, Toner, and other Jesuits were giving numerous workshops on communal discernment to groups of religious. During these same years, William J. Connolly, S.J., of the Center for Religious Development in Cambridge, Massachusetts, was in demand to conduct similar workshops and introduced me to the process when we facilitated such a workshop for all the Jesuit superiors of the New England province in 1972. In short order, I was asked to facilitate a number of such workshops in New England and abroad. A stint as vice provincial for formation took me out of circulation for such work until 1984, when, with Joseph McCormick, S.J., I was asked to work with the Jesuits of a large urban area to help them move toward communal discernment. What intrigues me is the silence about communal discernment since the surge of interest in the early 1970s that culminated in the call of GC 32. I suspect that attempts at communal discernment have foundered because the prerequisites were not present in groups.

Whenever I conducted a communal discernment workshop, I kept detailed process notes on what went on. I want to describe the process as I saw it with the hopes that such a description will be helpful to others. If the process of communal discernment has in fact fallen into disuse, perhaps we need a stimulus to revive it. In 1970, Futrell argued strongly that the times required a recovery of the Ignatian practice of communal discernment.

> If true communal discernment of experiments to enable the Society of Jesus to renew itself and to adapt to the signs of the times today is a condition for the survival of the Society in the modern Church, then it is vital that all Jesuits learn to engage in authentic Ignatian communal discernment.[9]

More than thirty years later, I believe the need is still present, and not just for Jesuits.

I have entitled this chapter "Toward Communal Discernment" deliberately. Many of the workshops in which I have participated have not reached the point of engaging in true communal discernment either because no question for discernment arose, or because of lack of time, or because other things needed to happen first. I suspect that many attempts at communal discernment falter for lack of the prerequisites outlined by both Futrell (1970 and 1972) and Toner (1971). Because both of these men have provided relatively detailed outlines of the actual process of discernment they use once these prerequisites are attained, I want to concentrate on the process of moving toward that attainment.

Communal discernment presupposes before all else that those who will engage in it have experienced the discernment of spirits in themselves. That is, each individual must have engaged in a process of contemplative prayer such as that proposed in the Spiritual Exercises, must have experienced the movements of the different "spirits," and must have discerned which movements are of God and which are not. Secondly, communal discernment presupposes that the individuals can and will communicate to others their experiences in prayer and in prayerful reflection. The ability to do so cannot be presupposed, because many of us were brought up in a tradition in which such communication was not only not encouraged but often enough actively discouraged. The recovery of the individually directed retreat and the development of a type of spiritual direction that requires the communication of religious experience are giving us the tools for the kind of communication communal discernment requires. But the willingness to communicate experience must also be present, and this is often the rock against which attempts at communal discernment shatter. Let me elaborate on this point.

When will any of us reveal our intimate selves to another person? Is it not when we trust the other not to laugh at or scorn or downplay our experience? Suppose that a person starts to tell me about an experience of prayer that meant something to her, and I swiftly change the subject or say, "That sounds odd to me." It will be a long time before she will take the chance again. When people approach a counselor for help because they are deeply troubled, they will test the waters with him or her before they reveal their intimate selves. In the same way, those beginning spiritual direction only gradually reveal the most intimate aspects of their relationship with God as they come to trust their spiritual directors. It is not easy to entrust our inner experience to others.

If this is the case in one-to-one relationships, how much more difficult is it to reveal ourselves in a group? Very often our reluctance to reveal ourselves comes from fear. What follows is a description of some of the processes we facilitators have used to help people in groups to overcome their fears and to entrust themselves more to one another.

First, we explain the role of the facilitators by an analogy to the role of the spiritual director. The spiritual director helps individuals to recognize their desires with regard to the Lord, to make these known to the Lord, and to put themselves into a receptive position so that the Lord's response may be heard. The spiritual director does not manufacture desires or prayer experiences for the other but helps the person to notice what is happening in the relationship with the Lord, to discern what leads toward the Lord, and to decide what to do about the discernment. So, too, the facilitators of the group try to help the group to articulate its desire as a group with regard to the Lord and to help the group to approach the Lord in prayer with that desire. Here it is important to remind individuals that they are asking the Lord to relate to them precisely as members of this group with the group's desire in mind; that is, to know that the Lord has hopes for *them* as a group. Just as individuals ask the Lord for what they desire, trusting that the Lord has their good at heart, so too the individuals in this group context approach the Lord with the group's desire, trusting that the Lord has the good of this group at heart.

The facilitators suggest a way for the members to approach, precisely as members of this group, the

Lord in personal prayer with the desire for the Lord's help. After the prayer period is over, they return to the group. The facilitators then help them to report to one another as much or as little as they wish to report of what happened during the prayer. Just as the spiritual director of an individual helps the person to notice and articulate as much as possible without judging what happened, so too the facilitators of a group ask the group to try to listen without judgment to the experiences shared. Indeed, because the assumption of such group sharing is that we are hoping to hear what God is saying to us as a group, these periods of sharing are approached, as far as possible, with the same contemplative attitude one hopes to have in private prayer.

Second, we point out that the process is a slow one of growing in trust in the Lord and in one another. Members already trust the Lord, but they probably have not thought much about the Lord's desires and hopes for the group. Most members of groups need to develop a trust in one another so that they see one another as deeply prayerful and honestly searching for God's will for the group. Communal discernment means that each member of the group trusts that God will reveal his will for the group through their individual prayer and through their sharing of the fruits of that prayer. To engage in this process, members must trust that all the others are sincerely praying and trying to remain open to discern God's will. After all, each person's future is on the line if he or she is willing to abide by the group's decision.

We usually structure the day into three sessions—morning, afternoon, and evening. The whole group gathers at the beginning of each session and we give them some orientation for private prayer. Each member prays for forty-five minutes to an hour and then takes a few minutes for reflection. If the group numbers less than ten members, all the sharing sessions are in one group. If the group is larger, we break it up into groups of ten or fewer for the sharing and ask that someone summarize for the whole group in a report. Each session, therefore, lasts at least two and a half hours. As the process goes on, we may have to vary the structure according to what is needed. For example, at the beginning of a session we may need to canvass the group to find out what its desire is.

Some groups begin the discernment process with much good will toward one another. Even so, members will still need time to develop the deeper trust in one another and in the Lord that this process requires. Suppose that such a group's purpose is to discover how they might best use their talent apostolically. Their numbers have declined, and they feel strained and overworked and realize that they can no longer continue to do all the work they have been doing. We would suggest they use for the first period of prayer a text such as Isaiah 43:1–5:

> Do not fear, for I have redeemed you;
>> I have called you by name, you are mine.
> When you pass through the waters, I will be with you;
>>> and through the rivers, they shall not
>>> overwhelm you;
> when you walk through fire you shall not be burned,
>> and the flame shall not consume you.
> For I am the LORD your God,
>> the Holy One of Israel, your Savior. . . .
> Because you are precious in my sight,
>> and honored, and I love you,
> I give people in return for you,
>> nations in exchange for your life.
> Do not fear, for I am with you.

We indicate that the Israelites heard these consoling words when they were in exile, when their temple was destroyed, and when their hopes were at their lowest. We suggest that they ask the Lord to give them a sense of hearing these words as applying to them as members of this group.

They then pray privately for forty-five minutes or so and afterward return to the group, where each member is asked to share whatever he or she wishes to share of what happened during the prayer. For most groups, such an icebreaker is reassuring, and the variety of experiences is enlightening. In a felt way, they realize how sincere and faith filled each one of them is. They are often surprised at how easy and enjoyable it is to talk about prayer with one another. Depending on how this first session goes, we might either suggest a repetition for the next session or suggest that they ask the Lord to help them to know the Lord's dream for them as a group. When we do move on to the latter point, we suggest private prayer in which each member asks God to reveal God's dream for them as a group.

During the group meetings, we remind them to listen to one another contemplatively and to note inner reactions as they listen. If they feel antipathy to what one member is saying, for example, they might want to ask the Lord's help to see things from that person's perspective. After the group has articulated its sense of God's vision and dream for them as a group, they might be ready to ask for the Lord's help to discover what blocks them from realizing the dream. Now the hard part begins, because they will be addressing neuralgic issues that may bring to light resentments, mistrust, and other "negative" emotions. The facilitators now begin to earn their keep.

Any group that has a history together has some bodies buried somewhere. We have been talking about groups who begin the process with much good will toward one another. Often enough, however, groups do not begin with much good will and trust. In these cases, the negative feelings may have to be addressed even earlier.

One group displayed so much anger, resentment, suspicion, and misunderstanding at the very first session that even the facilitators wondered whether they had opened Pandora's box. But we pointed out that their reality had surfaced rather quickly and suggested that they might feel as the apostles did after the Crucifixion when they boarded themselves up in the upper room. We asked them to imagine the apostles' feelings of guilt, anger, suspicion, and fear. And into their midst came Jesus, saying "Peace be with you." We suggested that they might want to spend an hour in prayer with this text (John 20:19–23) and then return. When they returned to the group, the atmosphere had noticeably shifted. Where before accusations and angry denunciations of others prevailed, now each one spoke of his or her own fears and failings and at the same time voiced a trust that the Lord would be with them as a group. We had not yet reached the

Promised Land, but we were on the way toward becoming a group that eventually might be able to engage in communal discernment.

In his 1972 monograph, Futrell makes a perceptive comment: "A community must have achieved the fruit of the First Week of the Spiritual Exercises *as a community* in order to begin true communal spiritual discernment."[10] He does not spell out what that might mean, but I believe that this prerequisite is crucial, and I believe that in at least one case I saw a group achieve that fruit. It was a group of male religious who were chapter delegates. They asked two of us to facilitate a four-and-a-half-day process that would help them toward being more discerning and open during the chapter that would follow. The congregation was reeling from a heavy financial blow and from departures that had left them demoralized, angry, and suspicious. Among the members of the group were some whom the others held responsible for their problems. Early in our sessions, feelings of anger, suspicion, guilt, and helplessness emerged. The first two days were stormy, but we could sense a gradual growth in trust. As one man said, "We have thought the unthinkable and said the unsayable."

Toward the end of the second day, we summarized the situation in this fashion:

You sense yourselves as broken, needy, helpless, and sinful precisely as members of this congregation and as chapter delegates. A number of you have identified with Simon the Pharisee who scorned Jesus for letting the sinful woman wash his feet. Some of you have voiced resentment at being put into the position of picking up the pieces of a mess caused by others. Some have voiced fears that as a group you will not have the courage to make the necessary decisions. Some fear that even God cannot change you. And yet you have also desired healing, have desired that Jesus make you brothers again. We suggest that you present yourselves to Jesus as you are and ask him for what you want. Perhaps you might want to do a repetition of Luke 7:36–50 or you might want to use the washing of the feet in John 13.

We also suggested speaking to Jesus on the cross and using the triple colloquy of the First Week of the Exercises.

The sharing after this period of prayer was very emotional and honest. One man asked with tears for the forgiveness of the group. Another reported emptiness in prayer and asked the group to pray for him. A couple of men said that the desire for healing was growing in them. Most of the others reported consolation and a sense of being healed. Tears were shed. At the end of the sharing, they broke up into dyads for reconciliation. The next day, men continued to ask one another for reconciliation. We spent the last two days focusing on Jesus' relationship with his apostles in the Gospel of Mark. At the end of the process, they felt hopeful and much more trusting as they prepared to enter their chapter. As a result of the "First Week experience," they seemed able to dream and to hope again as a group.

If spiritual directors need to have great trust in the Lord as their directees face some of the very painful and harrowing experiences sometimes associated with the process of conversion, such trust is even more imperative for those who facilitate groups toward communal discernment. It is all too easy to gloss over serious divisions in a group, to let sleeping dogs lie, as it were. It is all too easy to present techniques that can work only if prerequisites of trust and contemplative prayer are present. It is also all too easy to give up hope that the Lord can work wonders even on a group that at first seems hopelessly divided. Perhaps they do want to be healed as a group. I have never been a sole facilitator precisely because I feel the need for a companion so that together we can remind each other to pray, to entrust the group to the Lord, and to trust the good will of the group in spite of everything. After all, we say to each other, they have invited us to help them to become a discerning group, so they must have some hope in the Lord who has called them together. A group is close to becoming discerning when the members can say, as one man did, "During the Spiritual Exercises, I came to trust deeply that Jesus had a dream for me. Now I believe that he has a dream for us."

CHAPTER 12

Finding God in All Things: The Contemplation to Attain Love

Although there have been arguments throughout the history of the interpretation of the Spiritual Exercises about the place and importance of the Contemplation, I think that most contemporary commentators would agree with George Ganss that it is both "the conclusion and the apt climax of the spiritual experience of the Exercises."[1] However, we need to remind ourselves that this exercise is precisely a contemplation, not a meditation.

Ignatius does not expect that the fruit of this exercise will be attained by meditation on the four points of the Contemplation in the manner of the First Week's use of intellect, memory, and will to move oneself to the desired end. This exercise is called a "contemplation." Ignatius expects that retreatants will have arrived at the point where they desire experiences of God that will inflame their hearts with a greater love for God. Michael Ivens notes: "The word *attain* (in the title) is used in the sense not of 'obtain' but rather of 'reaching to' or 'arriving at.' The *love* to be 'attained' is a growing love on our part for God."[2] The desire of this contemplation is expressed thus: "to ask for interior knowledge of all the great good I have received, in order that, stirred to profound gratitude, I may become able to love and serve the Divine Majesty in all things" [n. 233]. Profound gratitude arises when I realize through God's grace that everything I have is gift, and gift undeserved; it is, perhaps, the foundational religious attitude and, Ignatius hints, it enables love for the giver to be born and to grow. Michael Buckley notes that this contemplation "aims at an elevation of consciousness, a growth in awareness, that kind of total human perception and experience which Ignatius called 'interior knowledge,' which caught up understanding, sensibility, and feeling."[3]

This interior knowledge, of course, is the response to divine revelation. Recall that in the Second Week, we ask for "an interior knowledge of Our Lord, who became human for me, that I may love him more intensely and follow him more closely" [n. 104]. Such an interior knowledge is not gained by study of the Gospels or of theology alone. We can only come to this kind of interior knowledge of another when the other chooses to reveal him- or herself to us. An interior knowledge of Jesus can only come if he reveals himself to us. Ignatius knew that the kind of love desired is an elicited love, a love that arises in a person because of the revealed interior loveliness of the other. As we shall see further on, the love Ignatius has in mind is a mutual love, a love that arises not so much because the other has been generous to us, but because we have come to know the other's loveliness and inner beauty. And we can only know that loveliness and beauty if the other reveals him- or herself to us.

It lies close to hand to see the text of this contemplation as the fruit of Ignatius's own mystical experiences at Manresa. He describes five of them in rapid succession in the *Autobiography,* beginning immediately after he has explained that "God was dealing with him in the same way a schoolteacher deals with a child while instructing him."[4]

> First. . . . One day . . . his understanding was raised on high, so as to see the Most Holy Trinity under the

aspect of three keys on a musical instrument, and as a result he shed many tears and sobbed so strongly that he could not control himself. . . . This experience remained with him for the rest of his life so that whenever he prayed to the Most Holy Trinity he felt great devotion.[5]

Second. One day it was granted him to understand, with great spiritual joy, the way in which God had created the world. He seemed to see a white object with rays stemming from it, from which God made light.[6]

Third. . . . One day, while in town attending Mass, . . . he saw with inward eyes, at the time of the elevation of the body of the Lord, some white rays coming from above. . . . He clearly saw with his understanding how our Lord Jesus Christ was present in that most holy Sacrament.[7]

Fourth. During prayer he often, and for an extended period of time, saw with inward eyes the humanity of Christ, whose form appeared to him as a white body, neither very large nor very small; nor did he see any differentiation of members. . . . These things that he saw at that time fortified him and gave such great support to his faith that many times he thought to himself: if there were no Scriptures, . . . he would still resolve to die for them on the basis of what he had seen.[8]

Fifth. [Facing the river Cardoner] . . . the eyes of his understanding were opened and though he saw no vision he understood and perceived many things, numerous spiritual things as well as matters touching on faith and learning, and this with an elucidation so bright that all these things seemed new to him.[9]

When Ignatius had these experiences, he was still a novice in the spiritual life; moreover, he was for all practical purposes innocent of any theological knowledge. His own experiences made him optimistic about what gifts others might receive from God. Ignatius expects that by the time people come to the Contemplation to Attain Love, they will have the desire for such personal revelations of God. As a result of this desire, they ask for an "interior knowledge." Ignatius, it seems, did not believe that he was singled out for the revelations he received because of any merit of his own; everything he received he considered a gift, and a gift that others could also desire of God. Ignatius expects that anyone can ask God for such a revelation and then hope that God will respond.

In fact, we could say that the desire for such revelation is only the correlative of God's desire in creating us. In *Let This Mind Be in You*, Sebastian Moore makes this point. In our case, the loveliness of the other awakens desire. But it is just the opposite with God. We do not exist until God desires us into existence. God desires us into existence and in so doing makes us desirable—to God. This creative touch of God that continually creates us and keeps us in existence evokes in us a correlative desire for God and for what God wants; namely, an intimate relationship.[10]

We are reminded of the famous lines of Augustine of Hippo's *Confessions:* "The thought of you stirs him [a human being] so deeply that he cannot be content unless he praises you, because you made us for yourself and our hearts find no peace until they rest in you."[11] Julian of Norwich, in her *Revelations of Divine Love,* echoes Augustine:

> Then we can ask reverently of our lover whatever we will. For by nature our will wants God, and the good will of God wants us. We shall never cease wanting and longing until we possess him in fullness and joy. Then we shall have no further wants.[12]

Julian has an even stronger image of God's thirst for intimacy with us near the end of her *Revelations:*

> For the thirst of God is to include Everyman within himself, and it is through this thirst that he has drawn his holy ones into their present blessedness. He is ever drawing and drinking, as it were, as he gets these living members, yet he still thirsts and longs.[13]

God's thirst for intimacy with us creates in us a correlative thirst. Ignatius experienced this thirst himself and presumed that he was not alone.

In his article in *The Way Supplement,* Michael Buckley writes of his belief that the four points of the Contemplation recapitulate the experience of the Four Weeks of the Exercises.[14] I believe that they can also be shown to recapitulate the interior meaning of the Principle and Foundation. The person now wants such a felt knowledge of the uniqueness of God and of God's intention in creation that it will be second nature to live in a spirit of gratitude and in tune with God's intention for the universe.

Before we look in more detail at the four points, let's spend some time on the two preliminary observations. The first reads, "Love ought to manifest itself more by deeds than by words" [n. 230]. Harvey Egan has demonstrated that the mysticism of Ignatius is a servant mysticism, a mysticism in service of God's project in creation.[15] In his monograph mentioned earlier, Joseph Tetlow shows convincingly that Ignatius's Principle and Foundation is based not so much on theological or philosophical theory as on experience, the experience of our continuing creation. He maintains that this experience is that we are being created momently by our God and Lord in all concrete particulars and that we are listening to God's summons into life when we let ourselves hear our most authentic desires, which rise out of God's passionate, creative love for us.[16]

One can argue that the purpose of the full Exercises is to help people to be so united with this creator God that they will want their actions to be in tune with God's intention at every moment of their lives. This is a large part of the importance of the discernment of spirits in the Exercises. By reminding people that love is shown in deeds more than in words, Ignatius is a mystic of action in tune with the one action of God. Even this Contemplation to Attain Love does not deviate from this perspective.

> Second. Love consists in a mutual communication between the two persons. That is, the one who loves gives and communicates to the beloved what he or she has, or a part of what one has or can have; and the beloved in return does the same to the lover. Thus, if the one has knowledge, one gives it to the other who does not; and similarly in regard to honors or riches. Each shares with the other. [n. 231]

What is extraordinary in this statement and in what follows it is this: Ignatius presupposes that God wants complete mutuality with us. He is talking about the Creator of the universe here, the God who needs nothing, who creates out of love, not necessity. Ignatius has discovered in his own experience that God wants mutuality, wants the love of friendship to obtain between God and himself and, therefore, between God and every human being. He found this discovery reinforced by his reading of Scripture and by his experience of directing others. Thus, God wants to be our dearest friend, our tremendous lover, and our beloved. God takes a terrible risk. God, by free choice, depends on our willingness to let God be our lover and our beloved; in other words, to let God be who God wants to be for us. If I do not choose to respond in mutuality, then God cannot be for me who God wants to be; namely, my beloved.

I have recently come to believe that God's intention for the universe, God's kingdom or rule, if you will, comes about not so much by heroic deeds of the saints, not so much by action to create a more just world, but by the willingness of each one of us to let God come close, to let God become our intimate friend. The rule of God comes about through friendship, through the love of friendship. As each one of us accepts this friendship, we are transformed. The more intimate we allow God to become, the more like God we become, or as the Greek theologians put it, the more "divinized" we become. Thus, our love becomes more universal and embraces all that God dreams for our world—a harmony of all people in a harmonious world. Such a view of things, it seems to me, locates the work of directing the Spiritual Exercises and of spiritual direction at the heart of the ministry of the church.

Let's now look more closely at the four points. In the first point, we ask to remember with deep affection all the gifts we have received both as part of the universe and of the human race and as a particular individual with a particular history. For those who have, during the time of the Principle and Foundation and the First Week, experienced their own salvation history, this point may give the Lord a chance to reinforce the revelation of that time. In fact, Michael Ivens indicates that this point may lead to a recalling of all the gifts received during the Exercises.[17]

Then Ignatius writes,

I will ponder with deep affection how much God our Lord has done for me, and how much he has given me of what he possesses, and consequently how he, the same Lord, desires to give me even his very self, in accordance with his divine design. [n. 234]

This is Ganss's translation. Other translations carry a further nuance in the last phrase. For example, Ivens translates it as "and further, how according to his divine plan, it is the Lord's wish, as far as he is able, to give me Godself."[18] As far as God is able. The poignancy in these words is palpable. God wants to give us all of Godself, but God cannot, both because we are not God and because we resist the gift.

To the extent that we experience such divine love and pathos, we can sing and mean St. Alphonsus Liguori's hymn "O God of loveliness." To the extent that we experience such divine love and let it penetrate our hearts, we will want to give all of ourselves to God and say with all our hearts, "Lord, I want to give you all that I am in return." Ignatius expresses this in his justly famous prayer:

> Take, Lord, and receive all my liberty, my memory, my understanding, and all my will—all that I have and possess. You, Lord, have given all that to me. I now give it back to you, O Lord. All of it is yours. Dispose of it according to your will. Give me love of yourself along with your grace, for that is enough for me. [n. 234]

Caught in the throes of such love, we have no fear of telling God anything or of entrusting God with our life and hopes and aspirations. We will not "seek health rather than sickness, wealth rather than poverty, honor rather than dishonor, a long life rather than a short one, and so on in all other matters." Rather, we will "desire and choose only that which is more conducive to the end for which we are created" [n. 23].

One of the more intriguing and challenging statements in Ignatius's *Constitutions of the Society of Jesus* says that those who are ill "show that they accept the sickness as a gift from the hand of our Creator and Lord, since it is a gift no less than is health."[19] To get some idea of how trusting Ignatius wants Jesuits to be, we can think of someone like Joseph McCormick, S.J., the former rector of the Jesuit community at Weston Jesuit School of Theology. This former spiritual director was also a retreat director to hundreds, a man of prodigious memory who used that gift for the sake of others. He suffered from Alzheimer's disease for the last five years of his life. "Take Lord, and receive . . . my memory." Can we really say that Joe's sickness was no less a gift than was his health and his wonderful memory? Apparently Ignatius could say so. Why? Because he had experienced God's self-revelation. He invites us to ask for the same self-revelation. Just recently, a woman in spiritual direction who had been experiencing the closeness of God for some time said that she no longer feared death; she felt that much desire for God.

In the Second Point, we ask to experience

> how God dwells in creatures; . . . and finally, how in this way he dwells also in myself, giving me existence, life, sensation, and intelligence; and even further, making me his temple, since I am created as a likeness and image of the Divine Majesty. [n. 235]

This point asks God to reveal to us how intimately related to everything in the universe God is. Let me just offer a thought here about what such a revelation might mean. We would experience how God is ingredient in this world, not only because of creation, but even more so because of the Incarnation. Our God is not the deist's god, who creates the universe and then leaves it to its own devices. Our God is always present in this universe, working out God's intention. But in addition, Jesus of Nazareth, a human being with physical, biological, psychological, sociological, and religious ties to the whole universe, is so at one with God that he is God. We believe in his bodily resurrection. This universe, therefore, is where God dwells forever.

In some real sense, this universe is heaven; the difference between now and after death is that our blinders will be removed, and we will see this universe for what it is—God's beautiful garden. In this Second

Point, we ask that our eyes be opened to this reality. If we have a deep experience of God's divine indwelling in all things, then we will indeed find God in all things and tend to reverence all things and people and ourselves. One who has such a deep experience will never want to misuse him- or herself or any other creature. Once again, we note how the Principle and Foundation is recapitulated, but now with a deeper, more mystical awareness of God's immanence in this universe.

In the Third Point, we ask to experience "how God labors and works for me in all the creatures on the face of the earth" [n. 236]. If God does reveal Godself so personally to us, then we will have an experience of God's one action in creating and sustaining the universe and will want with all our heart to live in tune with that one action. God is always acting in this universe to bring about what God intends. God is always trying to draw each of us and all of us together into God's own intimate Trinitarian life, that life that was called *perichoeresis* by the Greek theologians: "dancing around."

Frederick Buechner describes an experience of this "great dance that goes on at the heart of creation" occurring at an unlikely place, SeaWorld in Orlando, when on a beautiful day six killer whales were released into the tank.

What with the dazzle of the sky and sun, the beautiful young people on the platform, the soft southern air, and the crowds all around us watching the performance with a delight matched only by what seemed the delight of the performing whales, it was as if the whole creation—men and women and beasts and sun and water and earth and sky and, for all I know, God himself—was caught up in one great, jubilant dance of unimaginable beauty. And then, right in the midst of it, I was astonished to find that my eyes were filled with tears.

His wife and daughter had a similar experience. Buechner goes on to write:

I believe there is no mystery about why we shed tears. We shed tears because we had caught a glimpse of the Peaceable Kingdom, and it had almost broken our hearts. For a few moments we had seen Eden and been part of the great dance that goes on at the heart of creation. We shed tears because we were given a glimpse of the way life was created to be and is not. We had seen why it was the "morning stars sang together, and all the sons of God shouted for joy" when the world was first made, as the book of Job describes it, and of what it was that made Saint Paul write, even when he was in prison and on his way to execution, "Rejoice in the Lord always; again I will say, Rejoice." We had had a glimpse of part at least of what Jesus meant when he said, "Blessed are you that weep now, for you shall laugh."[20]

In the Third Point, Ignatius invites us to ask to experience this great divine dance that goes on at the heart of the universe.

Finally, in the Fourth Point we ask to experience "how all good things and gifts descend from above . . . just as the rays come down from the sun, or the rains from their source" [n. 237]. Here we find a clear echo of Ignatius's own mystical experiences as he described them in the _Autobiography._ If only we could experience all blessings and gifts as descending on us from above, then we would be able to live in spiritual poverty. We would be "indifferent to," "at balance toward" all created gifts and blessings because we would have intimate knowledge that these are only pale, though wonderful, reflections of the One "from whom all blessings flow," the One who is the deepest desire of our hearts.

Thus, people who come to this climax of the Spiritual Exercises come full circle. But now they know more intimately the Mystery we call God and in the process know themselves and their world more intimately. They are well on the way to being contemplatives in action, people who find God regularly in their actual lives of prayer and action. Indeed, for such people, prayer and action are not two different activities, but in some mysterious fashion one.

NOTES

Chapter 1
One Approach to Allowing "the Creator to Deal Immediately with the Creature and the Creature with Its Creator and Lord"

1. Gilles Cusson, *Biblical Theology and the Spiritual Exercises: A Method toward a Personal Experience of God as Accomplishing within Us His Plan of Salvation,* trans. Mary Angela Roduit and George E. Ganss (St. Louis, Mo.: The Institute of Jesuit Sources, 1988), 80.

2. Harvey Egan notes that Ignatius has a service mysticism, not a bridal mysticism. His spirituality cannot rest in union with God or Jesus alone unless it is union in service. Cf. Harvey D. Egan, *Ignatius Loyola the Mystic* (Collegeville, Minn.: Liturgical Press, 1991).

3. Harry Guntrip, *Psychotherapy and Religion* (New York: Harper, 1957), 194–195. The citation of Mackenzie is from *Nervous Disorders and Character.*

4. Cited in Harry Guntrip, *Psychotherapy and Religion*, 194–195. Of course, Ignatius would not agree that such enjoyment of God is the supreme end of spiritual

technique. For him, consolation had an orientation to action in accordance with God's will.

5. Cf. Sebastian Moore, *Let This Mind Be in You: The Quest for Identity through Oedipus to Christ* (Minneapolis: Winston, 1985).

6. Cf. C. S. Lewis, *Surprised by Joy: The Shape of My Early Life* (London: Geoffrey Bles, 1955).

7. C. S. Lewis, *The Pilgrim's Regress: An Allegorical Apology for Christianity, Reason and Romanticism* (New York: Sheed & Ward, 1944), 7–10.

8. In a monograph, Joseph Tetlow draws similar conclusions. Cf. "The Fundamentum: Creation in the Principle and Foundation," *Studies in the Spirituality of Jesuits* 21/4 (September 1989). "When I talk about creation here, I have in mind the In principio of John's prologue and the first chapter of Ephesians. Hence, I mean a different beginning, a beginning in no way limited by time or place but always ongoing in specific time and concrete place. When I talk about creation in these pages, I refer to God's constantly making each creature out of nothing at each moment of its existence, anteceding and causing all secondary causes" (4–5). We will deal more with the Principle in chapter 4.

9. There is an analogy here to the developmental stages of Erik H. Erikson and others. Cf. Erik H. Erikson, *Childhood and Society,* 2d ed. (New York: Norton, 1963), and for psychologists more influenced by Piaget, cf. Elizabeth Ann Liebert, *The Developmental Context of Spiritual Direction* (New York: Paulist Press, 1992).

10. For a helpful introduction to such counseling skills, cf. Gerard Egan, *The Skilled Helper: A Systematic Approach to Effective Helping,* 3d ed. (Monterey, Calif.: Brooks/Cole, 1986). For a further development of this approach to spiritual direction, cf. William A. Barry and William J. Connolly, *The Practice of Spiritual Direction* (HarperSanFrancisco: 1986).

11. Brian Moore, *Black Robe* (New York: E. P. Dutton, 1985), 246.

12. Leo Bakker, *Freiheit und Erfahrung: Redaktionsgeschichtliche Untersuchungen über die Unterscheidung der Geister bei Ignatius von Loyola* (Würzburg: Echter Verlag, 1970), 255 (translation mine). Harvey Egan makes a similar point in *The Spiritual Exercises and the Ignatian Mystical Horizon* (St. Louis, Mo.: The Institute of Jesuit Sources, 1976).

13. I am citing Gerard Manley Hopkins's poem "God's Grandeur."

14. Cf. William A. Barry and William J. Connolly, *The Practice of Spiritual Direction,* chapter 11.

Chapter 2
"What Do You Want?"

1. Sebastian Moore, *Let This Mind Be in You: The Quest for Identity through Oedipus to Christ* (Minneapolis: Winston, 1985).

2. In another context, I have discussed the courage of Bartimaeus. Cf. "Surrender: Key to Wholeness" in

Paying Attention to God: Discernment in Prayer (Notre Dame, Ind.: Ave Maria Press, 1990), chapter 6.

Chapter 4
The Principle and Foundation

1. Joseph A. Tetlow, "The Fundamentum: Creation in the Principle and Foundation," *Studies in the Spirituality of Jesuits* 21/4 (September 1989), 7.
2. In the section that follows, I borrow liberally from chapter 2 of my book *Finding God in All Things: A Companion to the Spiritual Exercises of St. Ignatius* (Notre Dame, Ind: Ave Maria Press, 1991).
3. Sebastian Moore, *Let This Mind Be in You: The Quest for Identity through Oedipus to Christ* (Minneapolis: Winston, 1985), 36.
4. C. S. Lewis, *Surprised by Joy: The Shape of My Early Life* (London: Geoffrey Bles, 1955), 22.
5. Frederick Buechner, *The Sacred Journey* (San Francisco: Harper & Row, 1982), 52.
6. Ibid., 56.
7. Anne Tyler, *Dinner at the Homesick Restaurant* (New York: Berkley Books, 1983), 284.
8. C. S. Lewis, *The Pilgrim's Regress: An Allegorical Apology for Christianity, Reason and Romanticism* (New York: Sheed & Ward, 1944), 7–10.
9. I develop the thought of John Macmurray and apply it to the encounter with God and to spiritual direction in *Spiritual Direction and the Encounter with God: A Theological Inquiry* (New York: Paulist Press, 1992).

10. Joseph A. Tetlow, "The Fundamentum," 8–9.

11. George E. Ganss, *The Spiritual Exercises of Saint Ignatius: A Translation and Commentary* (St. Louis, Mo.: The Institute of Jesuit Sources, 1992), 151.

12. Roger Haight, S.J., *Dynamics of Theology* (New York: Paulist Press, 1990), 153.

13. Ibid., 156–157.

Chapter 5
Transition Points in the Dynamic of the Exercises

1. Cf. Gerald G. May, *Addiction and Grace* (San Francisco: Harper & Row, 1988).

2. Cited in chapter 1 and quoted in Harry Guntrip, *Psychotherapy and Religion* (New York: Harper, 1957), 194–195.

3. Cf. Joseph N. Tylenda, *A Pilgrim's Journey: The Autobiography of Ignatius of Loyola* (Wilmington, Del.: Michael Glazier, 1985), n. 24.

4. For this insight, I am indebted to William J. Connolly, S.J.

5. John Macmurray, *Persons in Relation* (Atlantic Highlands, N.J.: Humanities Press, 1991), 171.

6. Cf. Edward E. Jones, Amerigo Farina, Albert H. Hastorf, Hazel Markus, Dale T. Miller, and Robert Scott, *Social Stigma: The Psychology of Marked Relationships* (New York: W. H. Freeman, 1984).

7. Ernest Becker, *The Denial of Death* (New York: Free Press, 1973).

8. From my own *Finding God in All Things: A Companion to*

the Spiritual Exercises of St. Ignatius (Notre Dame, Ind.: Ave Maria Press, 1991), 124–125.

9. John Macmurray, *Persons in Relation,* 171.

Chapter 6
Ignatian Contemplation

1. Joseph N. Tylenda, *A Pilgrim's Journey*, n. 8.
2. The Jesuit psychoanalyst William W. Meissner, in his psychobiography *Ignatius of Loyola: The Psychology of a Saint* (New Haven: Yale, 1992), shows rather convincingly that God's grace built on the psychic structure of Ignatius and that this psychic structure never disappeared.
3. Cf. M. Basil Pennington, *Centering Prayer: Renewing an Ancient Christian Prayer Form* (Garden City, N.Y.: Doubleday, 1980).
4. Cf. John Main, *The Heart of Creation* (London: Darton, Longman and Todd, 1988).
5. For a description of the kind of spiritual direction needed, cf. William A. Barry and William J. Connolly, *The Practice of Spiritual Direction* (HarperSanFrancisco: 1986).

Chapter 7
The Second Week and the Historical Jesus

1. Cf. Bernard Lonergan, *Insight: A Study of Human Understanding* (New York: Philosophical Library, 1957) and *Method in Theology* (New York: Herder and Herder,

1972). Specifically for scriptural study, cf. N. T. Wright, *Christian Origins and the Question of God,* vol. 1 of *The New Testament and the People of God* (Minneapolis, Minn.: Fortress, 1992), 29–144.

2. Cf. Brendan Byrne, "To See with the Eyes of the Imagination: Scripture in the Exercises and Recent Interpretations," *The Way Supplement* 72 (autumn 1991) for a very useful examination of the issues involved.

3. William A. Barry, *Who Do You Say I Am?: Meeting the Historical Jesus in Prayer* (Notre Dame, Ind.: Ave Maria Press, 1996).

4. John Meier, *A Marginal Jew: Rethinking the Historical Jesus,* vols. 1 and 2 (New York: Doubleday, 1991, 1994).

5. William A. Barry, *With an Everlasting Love: Developing an Intimate Relationship with God* (New York: Paulist Press, 1999).

6. N. T. Wright, *Christian Origins and the Question of God.*

7. N. T. Wright, "How Jesus Saw Himself," *The Bible Review* 12/3 (1996): 29.

Chapter 8
The Discernment of Spirits

1. Joseph N. Tylenda, *A Pilgrim's Journey,* nn. 15–16.

2. John Meier, *Mentor, Message, and Miracles,* vol. 2 of *A Marginal Jew* (New York: Doubleday, 1994), 415.

3. John Macmurray, *Freedom in the Modern World* (London: Faber & Faber, 1968). I have developed his thoughts

and tried to show that the discernment of spirits is a primary way to attain that maturity of heart. Cf. William A. Barry, *Spiritual Direction and the Encounter with God: A Theological Inquiry* (New York: Paulist Press, 1992), chapter 6.

4. Jospeh N. Tylenda, *A Pilgrim's Journey*, n. 45.

5. Ibid., n. 47.

6. Cf. Leo Bakker, *Freiheit und Erfahrung: Redaktionsgeschichtliche Untersuchungen über die Unterscheidung der Geister bei Ignatius von Loyola* (Würzburg: Echter Verlag, 1970).

7. Cf. Joseph A. Tetlow, "The Fundamentum."

8. Leo Bakker, *Freiheit und Erfahrung*, 105 (translation mine). In a recent article, João MacDowell makes the same point: "Ignatius gives a second function to consolation/desolation, thus making an original and inestimable contribution to Christian spirituality. He uses them (consolation/desolation) as elements for the discernment of the movements of the spirits and, through such discernment, for the discovery of the will of God in my regard: election." João A. MacDowell, "Nota Sobre as Noções de 'Moção,' 'Consolação' et 'Desolação' nos Exercícios Espirituais," Itaici: Cadernos de Espiritualidade Inaciana, 1 (1989): 51 (translation mine).

9. For a more extensive development of these ideas, cf. William A. Barry, *Spiritual Direction and the Encounter with God*.

10. Joseph N. Tylenda, *A Pilgrim's Journey*, n. 26.

11. Ibid., nn. 55, 82.

12. This is the felicitous phrase of George Aschenbrenner and far better expresses what Ignatius was about than the term *examination of conscience.* Cf. George A. Aschenbrenner, "Consciousness Examen," *Review for Religious* 31 (1972): 14–21. (Reprinted in David L. Fleming, ed., *Notes on the Spiritual Exercises of St. Ignatius of Loyola* [St. Louis, Mo.: Review for Religious, 1983], 175–185.)

13. William A. Barry, *Spiritual Direction and the Encounter with God,* 78.

14. Josef Sudbrack, "Unterscheidung der Geister— Unterscheidung im Geiste," in Kurt Niederwimmer, Josef Sudbrack, and Wilhelm Schmidt, *Unterscheidung der Geister: Skizzen zu einer neu zu lernenden Theologie des Heiligen Geistes* (Kassel: Johannes Stauda Verlag, 1972), 48.

15. Susan Howatch, *Glamorous Powers* (New York: A. A. Knopf, 1988), 57–58.

Chapter 9
The Changing Self-God Image of Ignatius in Relation to Discernment

1. I tried such a description in *Spiritual Direction and the Encounter with God,* chapter 5. There I define prayer as a conscious relationship and then attempt to describe the development of that relationship in terms of the dynamic of the Spiritual Exercises.

2. For an application of this theory to the relationship with God, cf. William A. Barry and William J. Connolly,

The Practice of Spiritual Direction, chapter 6.

3. Cf. Ana-Maria Rizzuto, *Birth of the Living God: A Psychoanalytic Study* (Chicago: University of Chicago Press, 1979).

4. Joseph N. Tylenda, *A Pilgrim's Journey,* n. 8.

5. Ibid., n. 15.

6. Ibid., n. 12 (italics mine).

7. Ibid., n. 19.

8. Ibid.

9. Ibid., n. 20.

10. Ibid., nn. 23–24.

11. Quoted in Harry Guntrip, *Psychotherapy and Religion* (New York: Harper, 1957), 195.

12. Tylenda, *A Pilgrim's Journey,* n. 23.

13. Ibid., n. 25.

14. Ibid.

15. Ibid., n. 26.

16. Ibid.

17. Ibid., n. 32.

18. Ibid., n. 33.

19. Ibid.

Chapter 10
Touchstone Experiences as Divining Rods in Discernment

1. William A. Barry and William J. Connolly, *The Practice of Spiritual Direction,* 103–104.

2. Andrew M. Greeley reports that more than half of his respondents admit to having had memorable religious

experiences. Cf. Andrew M. Greeley, *The Religious Imagination* (Los Angeles: Sadlier, 1981). In Great Britain, Alister Hardy's Religious Experience Research Unit at Oxford University has received thousands of examples of memorable religious experiences. Cf. Alister Hardy, *The Spiritual Nature of Man: A Study of Contemporary Religious Experience* (Oxford: Clarendon Press, 1979).

3. Alister Hardy, *The Spiritual Nature of Man: A Study of Contemporary Religious Experience,* 20.

4. Ibid., 21.

5. Ibid., 76–77.

6. Ibid., 34.

7. Ibid., 57.

8. Joseph A. Tylenda, *A Pilgrim's Journey,* op. cit., n. 30.

9. Cf. William A. Barry, *Paying Attention to God: Discernment in Prayer* (Notre Dame, Ind.: Ave Maria Press, 1990), chapters 4, 5, and 6 for a discussion of resistance to positive experiences of God.

Chapter 11
Toward Communal Discernment

1. Decree 11, "The Union of Minds and Hearts," of the Thirty-second General Congregation, para. 23. In *Documents of the Thirty-first and Thirty-second General Congregations of the Society of Jesus* (St. Louis, Mo.: The Institute of Jesuit Sources, 1977), 475.

2. Decree 8, "The Spiritual Formation of Jesuits," of the Thirty-first General Congregation, para. 124. In ibid., 108.

3. Ignatius of Loyola, *The Constitutions of the Society of Jesus,* trans. George E. Ganss (St. Louis, Mo.: The Institute of Jesuit Sources, 1970).

4. Joseph de Guibert, *The Jesuits: Their Spiritual Doctrine and Practice: A Historical Study,* trans. W. J. Young (Chicago: The Institute of Jesuit Sources, 1964).

5. John C. Futrell, "Ignatian Discernment," *Studies in the Spirituality of Jesuits* 2/2 (April 1970).

6. Jules J. Toner, "A Method of Communal Discernment of God's Will," *Studies in the Spirituality of Jesuits* 3/4 (September 1971).

7. John C. Futrell, "Communal Discernment: Reflections on Experience," *Studies in the Spirituality of Jesuits* 4/5 (November 1972).

8. Jules J. Toner, "The Deliberation That Started the Jesuits: A Commentary on the *Deliberatio primorum Patrum*: Newly Translated with a Historical Introduction," *Studies in the Spirituality of Jesuits* 6/4 (June 1974).

9. Futrell, "Ignatian Discernment," 70.

10. Futrell, "Communal Discernment," 169.

Chapter 12
Finding God in All Things

1. George E. Ganss, *The Spiritual Exercises of Saint Ignatius,* 183, n. 117.

2. Michael Ivens, *Understanding the Spiritual Exercises* (Leominster, Herefordshire: Gracewing, 1998), 172.

3. Michael Buckley, "The Contemplation to Attain Love," *The Way Supplement* 24 (Spring 1974): 95.

4. Joseph N. Tylenda, *A Pilgrim's Journey,* 36, n. 27.

5. Ibid., 36–37, n. 28.

6. Ibid., 37, n. 29.

7. Ibid., 37–38, n. 29.

8. Ibid., 38, n. 29.

9. Ibid., 38–39, n. 30.

10. Cf. Sebastian Moore, *Let This Mind Be in You: The Quest for Identity through Oedipus to Christ* (Minneapolis: Winston, 1985). This desire for "I know not what" is given the name "Joy" by C. S. Lewis in his autobiographical memoir, *Surprised by Joy.*

11. Augustine of Hippo, *Confessions,* trans. R. S. Pine-Coffin (Baltimore: Penguin, 1961), i, 1, 21.

12. Julian of Norwich, *Revelations of Divine Love,* trans. Clifton Wolters (Harmondsworth, England: Penguin, 1966), 71.

13. Ibid., 195.

14. Buckley, "The Contemplation to Attain Love."

15. Cf. Harvey D. Egan, *Ignatius Loyola the Mystic.*

16. Joseph A. Tetlow, "The Fundamentum," 7.

17. Michael Ivens, *Understanding the Spiritual Exercises.*

18. Ibid., 174.

19. *The Constitutions of the Society of Jesus and Their Complementary Norms* (St. Louis, Mo.: The Institute of Jesuit Sources, 1996), 120, [272].

20. Frederick Buechner, *The Longing for Home: Recollections and Reflections* (San Francisco: Harper & Row, 1996), 126–127.

Acknowledgments continued from copyright page

Quotations from the Spiritual Exericises are taken from George E. Ganss, trans., *The Spiritual Exercises of Saint Ignatius: A Translation and Commentary* (1992) and are used with the permission of the Institute of Jesuit Sources, St. Louis, Missouri. Permission is gratefully acknowledged.

The original form of chapter 1 was an address to an international symposium on the Spiritual Exercises convened by the Institut d'Etudes Théoligiques in Brussels in 1991 and was published in French in *La pratique des Exercices Spirituels d'Ignace de Loyola: Actes du Symposium de Bruxelles du 1er au 6 avril 1991*, copyright © 1991 by Editions de l'Institut d'Etudes Theologiques. Chapters 2, 3, 8, and 9 originally appeared in *Review for Religious*. A large section of chapter 6 first appeared as a chapter of *A Hunger for God*, copyright © 1991 by Sheed & Ward. Part of chapter 5 and the original form of chapter 7 appeared in *Human Development*. The original form of chapter 10 appeared in *The Way Supplement*. Permission to use these in revised form is gratefully acknowledged. I am grateful to Ave Maria Press for permission to reprint two sections of my book *Finding God in All Things: A Companion to the Spiritual Exercises of St. Ignatius* (1991), copyright © 1993, 2000 by the New England Province of the Society of Jesus.